CLOTHING
FOR THE
SOUL

CLOTHING
FOR THE
SOUL

WILLIAM R. KLEIN

PROVIDENCE HOUSE PUBLISHERS
Franklin, Tennessee

Printed in the United States of America

00   99   98   97   96   1   2   3   4   5

Library of Congress Card Number: 95-70538

ISBN: 1-881576-84-1

Cover by Bozeman Design

Published by
PROVIDENCE HOUSE PUBLISHERS
238 Seaboard Lane • Franklin, Tennessee 37067
800-321-5692

Contents

Preface   7

1. Clothing for the Soul   _v_   9
   Genesis 2:24–3:13, 21
   Romans 13:11–14

2. Quiet Agents of Grace   15
   Acts 9:1–10a

3. On Giving Hilariously   21
   Romans 8:31–32
   2 Corinthians 9:6–8

4. From Anger to Cynicism   27
   Micah 2:1–3; 3:1–2
   Matthew 9:32–33

5. "No One Comes to the Father But by Me"   33
   John 14:1–7

6. On Being Responsible for Our Lives   38
   Genesis 3:8–13
   John 5:39–40, 45–47

7. Life Can Begin Again *(p. 47)*   43 _v_
   Luke 19:1–10

8. Three Popular Misunderstandings of Faith   48
   Philippians 3:12–21 *(p. 51)*

9. Who Needs a Savior? *Sin & forgiveness*   53
   1 Timothy 1:12–17

10. Hearing the Gospel for the First Time   59
    Romans 5:6–11; 8:1, 35–39 *Nothing can separate us from the love of God*

11. God's Agenda and Ours   64
    Isaiah 55:8–11
    2 Corinthians 1:20–25

12. A Maundy Thursday Homily   69
    John 13
13. A Theological Question About Health Care   71
    Genesis 3:1–7
    Mark 2:1–12
14. Life Work *(the ware of The Lord)*   78
    Ecclesiastes 1:2–3; 2:4–6,18–21; 11:12b; 3:12–13
    I Corinthians 15:54–58
15. Reformed Spirituality *(guilty)*   84
    Colossians 1:9–14; 2:6–7
16. The Promise of Christmas   90
    John 1:14–18
    Romans 8:11
✳ 17. Understanding the Gospel   95
    Matthew 13:1–12
    1 Corinthians 2:14–16
18. A Colony of Heaven   101
    Matthew 18:20
    John 13:34–35
    Philippians 3:20–4:1
19. The Sacred Limits Others Pose for Us   106
    Ephesians 4:22–32
20. The Influence of Noble Human Beings   111
    Philippians 2:19–30
21. A Visit to Flossenburg   117
    Philippians 1:12–14, 20–21
Endnotes   123

Preface

SOME MONTHS AGO I ASKED THE MEMBERS OF SECOND Presbyterian Church, Roanoke, Virginia, to recommend sermons they would like to see published. The response was far more generous than I expected. I was also surprised by some of their suggestions. Some sermons which I would have rated very highly did not receive a single vote, while others which I would have gladly forgotten were quite meaningful to many. Such wisdom in God's people is surely a saving grace to preachers, and may also confirm Reuel Howe's suggestion that the sermon the Holy Spirit preaches in the hearing of the congregation is always better than the sermon the preacher writes and delivers. The sermons in this book represent, for the most part, the wisdom of this congregation.

I have a firm conviction that congregations have much more influence than they usually realize in the formation of a preacher. An unresponsive congregation can extinguish whatever fire may burn in a preacher's soul and reduce him or her, over a long period of time, to mediocrity. On the other hand, a congregation that values good preaching and supports a struggling preacher's efforts can fan embers into a flame and make a modestly gifted preacher slightly better than he might otherwise have been. It has been my good fortune to be cast into the midst of a congregation which tolerated my poor homiletical efforts when I first arrived at this pulpit twenty-eight years ago. Their patience and continued encouragement proved to be an instrument of the Holy Spirit.

It is to these patient and faithful people that I dedicate this book of sermons in the hope that as written words they may have a wider influence than the first hearing of them.

I have dedicated all proceeds from the sale of these sermons to the Second Presbyterian Church Fund, Inc. Perhaps in this way these sermons will have a more tangible influence on the future of this church.

A word of very special thanks goes to my dear friend Sue Deaton Ross (Mrs. William L.). The hours she spent proofreading my text significantly increased its quality. Her patience and support, no less important than her knowledge, are greatly valued.

—*William R. Klein*
Roanoke, Virginia

1

Clothing for the Soul

Genesis 2:24–3:13, 21; Romans 13:11–14

THE BIBLICAL TEXTS I HAVE CHOSEN FOR THIS MORNING, one from Genesis and the other from Romans, are about nakedness; the nakedness of the soul. They are also about clothing for our nakedness.

The first text is part of the story of Adam and Eve. Fresh from God's creative hand they are clothed in God's love and thus free to love him and each other in complete openness and trust. Thus clothed in God's grace they have nothing to hide from God, from each other, from their own souls; they are unashamed in their nakedness. But they rebel against God and cast off the robes of his grace. And suddenly they are shamefully aware of their nakedness and try pathetically to cover it.

Open your hearts to hear the ageless wisdom of this ancient story!

Adam and Eve were created for life together. For this reason the sacred text continues the story.

Therefore a man leaves his father and his mother and cleaves to his wife, and they become one flesh. And the man and his wife were both naked, and were not ashamed.

Now the serpent was more subtle than any other wild creature that the Lord God had made. He said to the woman, "Did God say, 'You shall not eat of any tree of the garden?'" And the woman said to the serpent, "We may eat of the fruit of the trees of the garden; but God said, 'You shall not eat of the fruit of the tree which is in the midst of the garden, neither shall you touch it, lest you die.'" But the serpent said to the woman, "You will not die. For God knows that when you eat of it your eyes will be opened, and you will be like God, knowing good and evil." So when the woman saw that the tree was good for food, and that it was

9

a delight to the eyes, and that the tree was to be desired to make one wise, she took of its fruit and ate; and she also gave some to her husband, and he ate. Then the eyes of both were opened, and they knew that they were naked; and they sewed fig leaves together and made themselves aprons.

And they heard the sound of the Lord God walking in the garden in the cool of the day, and the man and his wife hid themselves from the presence of the Lord God among the trees of the garden. But the Lord God called to the man, and said to him, "Where are you?" And he said, "I heard the sound of thee in the garden, and I was afraid, because I was naked; and I hid myself." He said, "Who told you that you were naked? Have you eaten of the tree of which I commanded you not to eat?" The man said, "The woman whom thou gavest to be with me, she gave me fruit of the tree, and I ate." Then the Lord God said to the woman, "What is this that you have done?" The woman said, "The serpent beguiled me, and I ate."

Genesis 2:24–3:13

So God drove Adam and Eve from the garden they had despoiled, and set a cherubim with flaming sword to bar their way lest they return to eat of the tree of life. But before they left Eden for a world filled with danger, "the Lord God made for Adam and for his wife garments of skins, and clothed them."

Genesis 3:21

Our New Testament text is from Paul's letter to the church at Rome. It tells of the royal robes God now provides to cover our nakedness and to protect us from the frigid power of sin and death.

Besides this you know what hour it is, how it is full time now for you to wake from sleep. For salvation is nearer to us now than when we first believed; the night is far gone, the day is at hand. Let us then cast off the works of darkness and put on the armor of light; let us conduct ourselves becomingly as in the day, not in reveling and licentiousness, not in quarreling and jealousy. But put on the Lord Jesus Christ, and make no provision for the flesh, to gratify its desires.

Romans 13:11–14

Most Presbyterians know by now that significant words in the Bible have much more than a literal meaning; they coax our imagination to ponder deeper realities. So whenever I teach the Book of Genesis and come to this third chapter, I always ask the class what the word "nakedness" suggests. Someone says, "vulnerable," and others follow suit (no pun is intended): "unprotected," "exposed," "defenseless." I always add that "nakedness" also has a positive connotation. It hints of "honesty," "truthfulness," "openness," "hiding nothing," "trusting one's very soul to another," especially to God from whom no secrets are hid.

The pure love of a husband and wife invites them to share physical nakedness without embarrassment and shame, even if their bodies are not the kind that swim-suit ads are made of. But deeper than this, pure love blesses us with such openness that we invite each other into the most private chambers of our souls where weaknesses and pretensions and fears, hidden from all other eyes, are trustingly revealed. To be clothed in such love and trust makes a man and a woman not only "one flesh" but one heart. And the worst of all blows to such love is for a spouse, in whose hands you have placed your very soul, to exploit your weaknesses, to publicly ridicule your secret fears and failings, to betray your trust. Few marriages are strong enough to survive such mortal wounds.

And if "nakedness" has this profound spiritual meaning, how shall we define the clothing that covers our nakedness? Is not such clothing that protects the soul's vulnerability the trust that grows with love, a sense of dignity and worth, the noble work of our hands and minds, and above all our trust in God's faithfulness? It is with just such things that God intends for us to cover our nakedness. And even when we turn against him and despoil his glorious creation, he still provides clothing to protect us out there in the jungle east of Eden.

It is the nature of sin to strip away everything that protects us: the trust that grows from love, a person's dignity and worth, the good we fashion with our hands and minds, our faith in God. "Sin is like stripping a tree of its bark, or an animal of its hide," writes Cornelius Plantinga, Jr., or a field of its vegetation and top soil. "To do these things is to remove the skin that protects against outside invaders" that destroy.[1] In our sin we strip our own souls of the things that cover our nakedness: Adam and Eve were not only ashamed, they were also terrified by the sudden onslaught of unexpected, dark forces that destroy psychic and spiritual wholeness. But our sin is perhaps most evident in the ways we despoil others and strip them of their dignity.

11

Professor Plantinga cites a story from Pierre VanPassen's book, *That Day Alone*.

Nazi troops capture a rabbi, force him to remove all of his clothing including his wedding ring, bend him over a barrel, and beat him numb with a leatherstrap. . . . Then they unfasten and display him. The soldiers ranged themselves in a semicircle around the table. One walked over and with a pair of scissors cut the left side of Rabbi Warner's hair away. Then he took hold of the Rabbi's beard and cut the right side of it away. Then he stepped back. The troopers laughed and slapped their sides.

'Say something in Hebrew,' the S.S. captain ordered. 'Thou shalt love the Lord thy God with all thy heart,' the Rabbi slowly pronounced in Hebrew. But one of the other officers interrupted him. 'Were you not preparing your sermon this morning?' he asked. 'Yes,' said the Rabbi. 'Well, you can preach it here to us. You'll never again see your synagogue; we've just burnt it. Go ahead, preach the sermon,' he cried out. 'All quiet now, everybody. Jacob is going to preach a sermon to us.'

'Could I have my hat?' asked the Rabbi. 'Can't you preach without a hat?' the officer asked him. 'Give him his hat!' he commanded. Someone handed the Rabbi his hat, and he put it on his head. The sight made the troopers laugh all the more. The man was naked and he was shivering. Then he spoke. 'God created man in his image and likeness,' he said. 'That was to be my text for the coming Sabbath."[2]

Why is it that some people take great delight in stripping away another's defenses: mocking, criticizing, belittling with sarcasm, ridiculing until one's soul spills out in tears? There was a junior high school teacher who took delight in humiliating her most lively and popular students. She would take a bright, happy, mischievous thirteen-year-old and humiliate him before the entire class. Aren't thirteen-year-old lads, the ones with the most promise, often the very ones who are mischievous? She was not happy until she'd shamed him into tears, and laughter could no longer dance in his eyes.

Why does a husband delight in ridiculing his wife before others, and why does the sight of pain in her eyes excite him to harsher ridicule? Why do some parents demand things of their children they cannot possibly do, and then fling their failures in their teeth until all sense of self-worth withers? Why do the rich and powerful assume they have the right to humiliate a waitress or a lowly employee who is defenseless, and who then brag to their cronies about making little people jump? And why does that waitress or employee go home and strip away with sarcasm and contempt whatever shreds of dignity their aged parents may still have until they wish they were dead? What is it about us that we have this demonic need to make a spectacle of others, beating them down until they're dehumanized?

"To despoil," says Dr. Plantinga, "is to wreck integrity or wholeness, to strip away what holds a being together and what joins it to other beings in an atmosphere of hospitality, justice, and delight. As Augustine shows in *The City of God*, sin despoils persons, groups, and whole societies. Corruption disturbs shalom, twisting, weakening, and snapping the thousands of bonds that give particular beings integrity, bonds that tie them to others."[3]

The point is made! Sin strips away the clothes that protect our naked souls from the deadly chill of nothingness. Sin also strips away the bonds that protect families and institutions and communities and societies from ancient hatreds, from greed, from fear, from apathy, from all the dark forces that destroy the spirit of community God intends for us poor, lonely creatures.

But what if it is true that in Jesus Christ God adorns our nakedness with such royal robes that we are shielded not only from the evil within our souls but from the evil that others would do to us? What if "putting on the Lord Jesus Christ" gives us such protection from sin, guilt and death that our wholeness is kept intact? No other garments can give us such dignity, for in "putting on Christ" we know we are the sons and daughters of God. And if we know who we are, how can we not act like royalty? It's like good Christian parents who raised their children to honor goodness, trust and integrity. When their lovely daughter went off on her first high-school prom, all they had to say was simply, "Remember who you are!" That is but an echo of Peter's reminder to all Christians: "You are a chosen race, a royal priesthood, a holy nation, God's own people . . ."[4] Remember who you are and you will be clothed with might!

So the story is told of a medieval monk, a rare and gifted scholar who served Jesus Christ his Lord by translating ancient scriptures and texts. Once, on a visit to Paris, he was set upon by brigands who dragged him into an alley, stripped him and beat him and left him for dead. He was found and taken to a public clinic of sorts. In that age, professionally educated people generally spoke Latin, so the attending physician looked at this half-dead monk, assumed he was an ignorant beggar, and not wanting to be understood, said to his colleague, in Latin: "We will not waste our time on this worthless creature." Mustering his last ounce of strength, this monk raised his head and whispered in flawless, classic Latin: "Never call

13

worthless anyone for whom Christ died."

Thus clothed with the ultimate dignity Christ gives, not only are we protected from the frigid blasts of self-accusation and self-hatred which so often assault our poor souls and which we frantically try to mask; not only are we protected from guilt and despair and death; we also are set free from that demon that drives us to humiliate others. Indeed, if we know the forgiveness and love of Jesus Christ, we do even more: It becomes our joy to affirm the dignity and worth of others, for Christ's sake. So the greatest compliment anyone can pay a Christian is not, "Her virtue is so great!" or "His knowledge is so great!" or "Her moral courage is an example to all!" but simply this: "When I am in her presence I am strangely aware of another Presence and I believe I can somehow be better than I ever dreamed!"

So tell me, do you still think the smelly rags your pride stitches together can really hide your nakedness? Or has the grace of Jesus Christ covered your nakedness and given you such security that you can be his faithful servant, sowing goodness where there is evil and hope where there is despair?

Let us join our voices as we pray in unison the great prayer of St. Francis of Assisi.

O Lord our Christ, may we have Thy mind and Thy spirit; make us instruments of Thy peace: Where there is hatred, let us sow love; where there is injury, pardon; where there is discord, union; where there is doubt, faith; where there is despair, hope; where there is darkness, light; and where there is sadness, joy. O Divine Master, grant that we may not so much seek to be consoled as to console; to be understood as to understand; to be loved as to love; for it is in giving that we receive; it is in pardoning that we are pardoned; and it is in dying that we are born to eternal life. Amen.

2

Quiet Agents of Grace

Acts 9:1–10a

OUR STORY FROM THE BOOK OF ACTS IS ABOUT TWO men. The name of one is very familiar; the name of the other is hardly ever mentioned. Everyone knows who Paul was, but very few ever heard of Ananias. But if it hadn't been for Ananias, there's a good chance we'd never have heard of Paul.

We first hear of Paul as a young adult in Jerusalem. He was known as Saul back then. He joined the mob that stoned Stephen, the first Christian martyr. And from that day on his reputation grew as a violent enemy of Christ and his church. But our Lord Jesus had other plans for this Saul of Tarsus. Listen to one of the great stories in the New Testament!

But Saul, still breathing threats and murder against the disciples of the Lord, went to the high priest and asked him for letters to the synagogues at Damascus, so that if he found any belonging to the Way, men or women, he might bring them bound to Jerusalem. Now as he journeyed he approached Damascus, and suddenly a light from heaven flashed about him. And he fell to the ground and heard a voice saying to him, "Saul, Saul, why do you persecute me?" And he said, "Who are you, Lord?" And he said, "I am Jesus, whom you are persecuting; but rise and enter the city, and you will be told what you are to do." The men who were traveling with him stood speechless, hearing the voice but seeing no one. Saul arose from the ground; and when his eyes were opened, he could see nothing; so they led him by the hand and brought him into Damascus. And for three days he was without sight, and neither ate nor drank. Now there was a disciple at Damascus named Ananias. The Lord said to him in a vision, "Ananias." And he said, "Here I am, Lord." And the Lord said to him, "Rise and go to the street called Straight, and inquire in the house of Judas for a man of Tarsus

15

named Saul; for behold, he is praying, and he has seen a man named Ananias come in and lay his hands on him so that he might regain his sight." But Ananias answered, "Lord, I have heard from many about this man, how much evil he has done to thy saints at Jerusalem; and here he has authority from the chief priests to bind all who call upon thy name." But the Lord said to him, "Go, for he is a chosen instrument of mine to carry my name before the Gentiles and kings and sons of Israel; for I will show him how much he must suffer for the sake of my name." So Ananias departed and entered the house. And laying his hands on him he said, "Brother Saul, the Lord Jesus who appeared to you on the road by which you came, has sent me that you may regain your sight and be filled with the Holy Spirit." And immediately something like scales fell from his eyes and he regained his sight. Then he rose and was baptized, and took food and was strengthened.

Acts 9:1–10a

Ananias is surely one of the great unsung heroes of the New Testament. Had he refused to welcome Saul, the history not only of the church but also of western civilization would have taken a far different course.

The biblical narrative gives no hint of it, but I rather think there was a long pause as Ananias pondered if he should do this. What if he had misunderstood what he'd thought was God's voice? After all, this was one of the church's worst enemies. And it was rumored that he was coming to Damascus to ferret out the followers of Christ. What if he welcomed Saul, introduced him to his fellow believers, and it turned out to be a clever ruse? The Christian community in Damascus would be wiped out, and he would carry the burden of that guilt to his grave.

But that unthinkable word of God kept prodding him. It made no sense, but then God doesn't always limit his gracious dealings to the logic of our Euclidean minds. So Ananias set out to find the street called Straight, not with head erect but bent over like an old man trudging up a long, steep hill. I can see him half way there, stopping and turning around and heading back home shaking his head, only to stop again with God's command ringing in his soul, and slowly putting one foot in front of another until he turned onto the street called Straight and stood at the door of a man whose name was Judas. That morning's walk had been the longest Ananias had ever made.

He took a deep breath, opened the door, and saw for the first time that dreaded enemy of the church. The form before him was not that of a fearsome enemy, but of a sad, broken, helpless man whose world had been shattered. He even felt a twinge of pity for this evil zealot. "Brother Saul!" he whispered.

"Brother?" He could hardly believe his own words. But for Saul to be called "brother" by one who had every reason to loath him was almost as great a miracle of grace as the voice of Jesus he had heard on the road.

Yes, Ananias is one of the great, unsung heroes of the New Testament and of the church, for had he not risked everything to be an agent of God's grace, how different, how sadly different, our world and we ourselves would be. Life is like this. The great turning points in our lives seldom come in thunderous events, with trumpets blaring, but with a touch on our shoulder or a quiet voice which calls us "brother" or "sister" or simply "friend."

It was like this for Saint Augustine, "the greatest of the early church theologians, who was given the honorific title Doctor Gratia, Doctor of Grace.[1] There was another man, an older contemporary of Augustine. His name was Ambrose, Bishop of Milan, an important man in his own right but far less widely known and respected than the great Augustine eventually would be. St. Augustine said that it was Ambrose who won him to Christ. Years afterward St. Augustine said, "I began to love my teacher Ambrose, not at first as a teacher of the truth, which I despaired of ever finding in the church. Instead, I loved him simply as a fellow creature who was kind to me."[2]

Each of us could tell similar stories, of someone's kindness and encouragement that sent us in a new and happy direction. A chance meeting with an old friend when you're feeling that your life's amounted to nothing, and she tells you how the example of your life gave her inspiration to keep going when she wanted to give up. That's like sunlight flooding the musty cellar of your soul, and suddenly it's easier to smile again. A friend recommends a book he thinks you'll enjoy, and as you read something clicks, and a new understanding of life and how you fit into it turns you completely around. Someone says, "Why don't you ask So-and-So for a date?" So you ask with trepidation and discover she's the girl of your dreams and a new, lifelong love carries you both into a future neither of you would have known had that friend not dropped a suggestion. Or maybe there's a job opening somewhere you know nothing about. All you know is that your present job has drained your spirit dry and the challenge has gone out of it. But a friend suggests you for the opening, an offer is made, and you and your family go to a new city to start a new and different life.

It was like that with me, as some of you know. Marc Weersing, who'd been my minister when I was a high school student in Atlanta, was invited to preach here for your Seventy-Fifth Anniversary. Dr. Hollingsworth had announced his retirement from this pulpit, and this friend, unbeknown to me, suggested to your Pulpit Committee that it might be worth their while to drive down to Rock Hill, South Carolina. And here I am, twenty-seven

17

years later. And these have been the most satisfying, the most productive years of my life.

All of us have had such unexpected gifts, for that's exactly what they are. Quiet agents of God's grace have opened up new vistas that changed our lives forever. In our library at home is a book entitled *Mothers of Famous Men*. I'm sure somewhere there's a book entitled *Fathers of Famous Women*. Nonetheless, show me anyone whose life and work have made this world a little better, and you'll find behind that great human being a mother whose prayers and words of wisdom instilled in his young soul a sense of decency and honor, and the conviction that greatness is found in serving others. For some it may have been a father's example. The great philosopher Immanuel Kant recalled his childhood years when his father's business interests suffered greatly from unfair competition from those he had trusted. Kant said, "Even in the conversation of the family the quarrel was mentioned with such forbearance and love toward the opponents that the thought of it, though I was only a boy then, will never leave me."[3]

You might say that the forgotten, lesser person, a mother, a father, a friend, launched the greater person. But in the long run who is to say which is lesser and which is greater? Who was the humble preacher who launched Billy Graham on his evangelistic career? Was there a country doctor who planted the vision of medicine in the hearts of Charles H. Mayo and his brother William? Was it a mother's love of words and the sheer beauty of the English language that first led T. S. Elliot to dream of writing? Who can say that the roles of those forgotten people are unimportant? No one is unimportant who is an agent of God's grace.

Ananias and Ambrose, and all the people whose acts of kindness have influenced us and others for good, were only doing what Jesus did again and again. During the years when Jesus first walked the hills of Galilee, no one saw him then as the Savior of the world, only as an unusual man who "went about doing good and healing all who were oppressed. . . . "[4] Zacchaeus wanted only a glimpse of him and climbed a sycamore tree to get a look at this man of simple kindness. The nameless woman with the uncontrollable bleeding only wanted to reach out and touch the hem of his robe, so quietly that no one would notice. Another nameless woman came in off the street when Jesus was in the house of Simon the Leper and anointed Jesus' feet with ointment. She simply wanted to express her devotion. Or think of the countless, nameless people who came to Jesus to hear his gracious words or to feel his healing touch. He was kind and gracious to each of them, and they all left his presence feeling better about themselves and about life, and somehow closer to God.

John tells of Jesus' meeting with a Samaritan woman who had come to Jacob's well to draw water.[5] While the narrative is so simple a child can follow it, John, always the master artist, deftly weaves into it deep theological undertones about marriage and worship and the water of life, themes that challenge the most learned. On the surface, however, the story is about a Samaritan woman, an outcast whom no self-respecting Jew would deign to engage in public conversation. But Jesus talked to her in public. And on top of that her morals left much to be desired. She'd had five husbands, and her current "significant other" shared her bed without benefit of clergy. Yet Jesus was not judgmental nor did he moralize, as we, the self-appointed defenders of pure morals are wont to do. He simply treated her with courtesy and respect. And she was so impressed that in her excitement she left her water bucket and ran back to town to tell everyone of the remarkable man she had just met.

The Samaritan woman, Zacchaeus, the woman with the uncontrollable bleeding, the woman who soothed his road-weary feet, the countless, nameless people who met him and then dropped from sight. We have no idea whatever became of them. "Whether these and others who came into contact with Jesus became disciples or believers, they apparently experienced the divine presence in their midst and found, in the process, a new sense of self worth."[6] What a difference they must have made to all they henceforth touched.

I came across a marvelous verse of scripture the other day. I'd read it many times, but it never snagged my attention. It's in the Ninth Chapter of Hebrews. "Christ appeared as a high priest of the good things that have come. . . . "[7] "*As high priest of the good things that have come.*" Is there any reason why we shouldn't believe that Christ, the high priest of good things, is the hidden presence in the words and deeds of those who nudged us to enter a life of joy and meaningful service to others? Is there any reason why we shouldn't believe that this Christ is the hidden presence in anyone, anywhere whose quiet acts of kindness and love lead people to new and better lives? And can we not believe that Christ our high priest takes all our imperfect deeds and words of goodness into his hands, makes them better by his perfect love, and uses them to achieve more than we could ever dream of?

There are many ways to measure greatness: wealth, fame, artistic creativity, inventiveness. But perhaps the supreme measure of greatness is seen in those humble enough and loving enough to be the quiet instruments of God's grace. This will not likely make us the richest or the most successful person around, but it will make us something better: a human being in the purest sense.

A few moments ago I spoke of the change in all those nameless people who came in contact with Jesus. They went away with a new feeling of self-worth. Because of Jesus they knew they had dignity and the grace to be better than they were. What greater gift can any of us give to another!

I have two very dear friends who served together in the same church. The younger was the senior minister; the older was the associate pastor. It was said of the senior minister that everyone respected and admired him. He was and is an outstanding leader in the church. But it was said of the associate pastor that everyone loved him for the simple reason that all who came in contact with him, the poorest and the richest, went away feeling better about themselves.

If you and I can be such quiet agents of God's grace that all who meet us can go away feeling good about themselves and believing that life can be better than it is, then we will have achieved a greatness even the angels will envy. And you can be such an agent, through Christ our Lord, the high priest of good things—starting this very moment.

3

On Giving Hilariously

Romans 8:31–32; 2 Corinthians 9:6–8

LEST I FALL INTO THE HANDS OF LAWYERS AND BE SUED for plagiarism, I want to own up to the source of my sermon title. I got it from a sermon by Robert J. McCracken, minister in the 1950s of the great Riverside Church of New York City. Such a title is too good to go to waste in a dusty old book of sermons.[1] Our first text is from Romans. It tells of the extravagant love of God for you and me.

> What then shall we say to these things? If God is for us, who can be against us? He who did not spare his own Son, but delivered him up for us all, how shall he not with him also freely give us all things?"
>
> *Romans 8:31–32*

Our second text is from Second Corinthians. It's part of Paul's steward-ship letter to the Christians of Corinth. Paul knew that the secret of giving cheerfully, even hilariously, belongs only to those blessed ones who have caught a little of God's extravagant love in Christ Jesus our Lord. He wanted his friends in Corinth to be filled with the same spirit.

> So the point is this: He who sows sparingly will also reap sparingly, and he who sows bountifully will also reap bountifully. Each one must do as he has made up his mind, not reluctantly or under compulsion, for God loves a cheerful giver. And God is able to provide you with every blessing in abundance, so that you may always have enough of every-thing and may provide in abundance for every good work.
>
> *2 Corinthians 9:6–8*

Remember the story about the little boy who emptied his piggy bank and bought two yellow roses for his mother? How could she scold him for such

21

reckless extravagance? It was his gift of love, filling her heart and his with a momentary, unforgettable burst of joy. What if she'd ruined that enchanted moment, asking how much he'd spent, or advising him to be more prudent in the future?

Such extravagant love is admirable in little boys, but not in grown men or women with bills to pay and responsibilities to keep. In order to survive in our cold world, little boys and little girls must learn to rein in their generosity, to save wisely, and to manage money prudently. But what if the cost of acquiring such prudence is the loss of a certain generosity of spirit without which love is joyless?

"If prudence is a prime virtue in our world," wrote Edmund Steimle, "extravagance is the word for God."[2] The heart of God is the most extravagant of all hearts, holding nothing back but endowing us and this world with beauty and joy and riches beyond measure, even giving his beloved Son so we can be free to live joyfully and lovingly. "He who did not spare his own Son but gave him up for us all, will he not also freely give us all things with him?" Do not miss Paul's logic! As Thomas F. Torrence reminds us, "God has revealed that he loves us more than he loves himself."[3] If God's love for us is such that the giving of his only Son was like ripping out his own great heart, can he not be trusted to do the easier thing of freely giving us whatever we need to embrace that love?

So it was to fashion human hearts after this extravagant, even reckless heart of God that Jesus came to live among us. That's what stewardship is about—not dollars and cents, but coaxing into life in these tight-fisted little hearts of ours a spirit that loves and gives freely, even recklessly. But, God forgive us, we do not hear; we do not understand. We keep God at a safe distance by insisting that stewardship is dollars and cents or accurate bookkeeping or paying off spiritual debts or badgering people to give more until it hurts. How frigid!

A few examples of the way we put our cold, leprous hands on this extravagant love which God keeps trying to coax into life on the barren landscape of our souls!

Remember Jesus' story about contributions for the temple? Into the huge golden offering bowls the rich folks dropped big bills, holding them high and letting them float down for all to see. And along came a poor widow who put in two little copper coins, very quietly, I'm sure, because she didn't want to be embarrassed by the tinny sound of copper on gold. But no gift was given that day with greater love and joy.

Are you surprised that Jesus was unimpressed with the other gifts, with the kinds of gifts college fund raisers list along with the names of the donors in "The Century Club" or some similar honorific classification? It was the extravagant, even reckless gift of that poor widow that sent a tremor through his great heart, for here was a woman whose heart was akin to the heart of God.

Lesser men and women can only ask, "How much?" And while they may tip their hats at the widow's gift, only because Jesus told the story, not because they really believe it represents the essence of stewardship, they would likely advise Jesus to come down harder on folks. "Make them feel guilty because they're not giving enough, and tell them how much it costs these days to keep the Temple open and running. That's what stewardship sermons are made of. Of course, your admiration for widows and their gifts is certainly a noble sentiment, Mr. Jesus, but if you keep singing that tune the Temple will soon be out of business."

How quickly extravagant love turns damp and moldy under our careful calculations of less and more. And the point is not that large gifts are unimportant or unappreciated. It's just that in terms of stewardship, the dollars-and-cents people always start at the wrong end. Give me a thousand hearts that love with glorious abandon like that little boy or that poor widow—that's the end where Jesus always started—and we can retire our Stewardship Committee and still have more money than we'd know what to do with.

God is not very interested in the size of our gifts, only in the kind of hearts growing within us. For if, by the grace of God, we are beginning to learn, however falteringly, to love and to give as he does, we will keep on learning, until in his heaven we will know unceasingly the kind of joy that held that little boy and his mother together for a moment of splendor, and the kind of glory Jesus saw in that widow's adoring gift of all she had.

⸙ A second example of the moldy blight we put on the extravagant love of God! We all know the extravagance of God in the splendor of nature: the dazzling splash of colors in a spring garden or an autumn hillside, the shimmering light of a full moon on a quiet sea, a breath-taking sunset, the pure innocence in the face of a new-born child. Allan Watts once wrote that the extravagance of nature is like music at its highest and best.

> The preludes and fugues of Bach, he writes, are simply a complex arrangement of glorious sounds. . . . They need no programme notes to explain a moral or sociological message. . . . The intricate melodies flow on and on, and there never seems any necessity for them to stop. He composed them in tremendous quantities, with the same God-like extravagance to be found in the unnecessary vastness of nature. [4]

23

Music, with its infinite variety, can point our beggarly hearts heavenward and lift them to the stars. Do you really think a stingy, tight-fisted God could have endowed the human spirit with such talent for beauty? There's a story about Satan. After he rebelled against God and was cast out of heaven, he was asked aeons later what it was he missed most. "The sound of trumpets in the morning," he said. [5]

But we poison this delightful gift of God's love with our psychological and sociological analyses, just as money counters poison gifts of the heart. No longer can you simply revel in the beauty of a Brahms symphony! Now its music must be analyzed for its hidden expressions of cultural superiority or ethnic pride or sexist oppression, not to mention its setting in an age far inferior to ours. We call this crude dissection of beauty "intelligence." And suddenly, like the blight our miserly hearts cast upon a little boy's love, the music that opens the windows of the soul to the majesty of God becomes soundless. Even Satan knew the sound of trumpets was nothing if not the awakening of the soul to God's glory.

I've heard it said that there's no singing in hell either. I have no hard facts, only a hunch, but I'll wager that hearts that do not sing, if only in a joyful monotone, are also hearts that do not give extravagantly either!

One more example of God's love!

If nothing else is said of God's forgiveness, it is extravagant, never giving up, always reaching out to lift up his fallen children, reaching out even to those who murdered his beloved Son. There is no sin of which we are capable which is beyond the reach of God's forgiveness, except the sin against the Holy Spirit, as Jesus called it. And what is that except our proud refusal of God's proffered love, our cynical rejection of whatever light we may have within us, and our willful repudiation of any sense we may have of our emptiness and need of God. But then, it is not that God withdraws his offer of forgiveness, but that we render our souls so calloused and hard that the love of God can no longer move us. But for those who open their proud hearts to God's gift of forgiveness, life is new again, full of joy and promise, and the trumpets greet each new day. And one thing more! Having been forgiven, we catch something of God's spirit, and we begin to learn, however imperfectly, to forgive others as freely as we have been forgiven.

But we poison this extravagant gift of God's forgiveness with our pious legalisms, and with our rigid laws of right and wrong which we use so piously to condemn our brothers and sisters. "God, I thank thee," said the loveless Pharisee, "that I am not like other men."[6] Why are the self-righteous always so brittle and loveless? No wonder that Pharisee saw Jesus and his forgiveness as a deadly threat to his own narrow little kingdom of self-righteous achievements!

That Pharisee, and his spiritual descendants in every generation, so exercised their own moral muscles that they became hard and sinewy, like that bird in the children's cartoon called "Road Runner." You wouldn't serve "Road Runner" on your Thanksgiving table. There'd be no succulent meat on his dry bones, only tough tendons you'd spit out and feed to the swine. The morally self-righteous are always like that. No one can swallow them because they forever hold up in your face your past sins and mistakes, and they will drag them out for others to see whenever it serves their purpose. And if you find in this a hint of the recent political trench warfare, you are welcome to make that connection.

To such infallible moral bookkeepers God's forgiveness is always scandalous, love wasted shamefully on the unworthy and the undeserving. But God has this amazing way of not being overly concerned about past sins. He is much more concerned about the persons we are becoming, and to free us from the burden of past sins and to keep us ever reaching for tomorrow and the person we can be, he forever lavishes his forgiveness upon us. How else can we explain his willingness to keep seeking us out and lifting us up when we fall? And what is more, such budding saints as we are, are learning, however imperfectly, to be generous in the forgiveness of others.

Again I have no hard facts, only a hunch, but I'd wager that those who are stingy forgivers are stingy givers in everything else as well. They are incapable of hilariously giving themselves, their love, their praise, or their wealth.

Well, this is the only kind of stewardship sermon I know how to preach and remain faithful to the gospel, for stewardship, as Jesus understood it, is not about dollars and cents, but about the joyful giving of one's self in the service of God and his kingdom.

What kind of person are you becoming, by the grace of God? What kind of person do you want to become, by the grace of God? I pose this question to myself and I ask where I should look in my life to find the real me that is coming into being. Do I see the person God is fashioning in me in those rare moments when I fling open the windows of my heart and love extravagantly, or in the dull humdrum of daily existence when I am fearful of life and the future and tell my timid little soul that I must be cautious and prudent? Do I catch a fleeting glimpse of the person I really want to become in those rare and beautiful moments when my heart leaps up at the music of the spheres and the joy of being forgiven floods my soul, or when I am so serious with doubts and unanswerable questions that I feel as if the dreams that tug at my soul are only pipe dreams? Do I know who I really am in those rare moments when I wish I could be like that little boy who raided his piggy bank in a joyful burst of love's abandon, or in those moments when I listen to the world's prudent advice about carefully guarding my precious dollars?

And you? What do you think you might do to yield a willing hand and a compliant heart to God so he can begin his gracious work of transforming you into a hilarious, extravagant giver like himself? Maybe you could pick up that pledge card, if you feel happy about it. And if you've already turned one in, you could maybe turn in a new one, but only if you feel happy about it. I mean, you don't have to be a genius to know that "he who sows sparingly will also reap sparingly, and he who sows bountifully will also reap bountifully." But you must do it, "not reluctantly or under compulsion, for God loves a hilarious giver."

4

From Anger to Cynicism

Micah 2:1–3; 3:1–2; Matthew 9:32–33

ANGER CAN BE HEALTHY AND CONSTRUCTIVE, OR IT can be sick and destructive. The justified anger that gave rise to "Mothers Against Drunk Drivers" has benefited all of us. But lust for vengeance, especially when it masquerades as righteous indignation, drives us to overreact destructively. Think of the incarceration of Japanese Americans after Pearl Harbor, or of the distrust of Muslims because of Arab terrorists. Cynicism, on the other hand, is never healthy or constructive. "Caution," "suspicion," yes, but never cynicism, for cynicism denies the very existence of virtue and truth. The sermon explores how anger leads to cynicism.

I have chosen two texts that show how cynicism kills our sensitivity to the good, the loving, the pure. The first text comes from the prophet Micah. Listen to God's judgment upon the powerful in Israel, so blinded by greed they made injustice and evil their crowning virtue.

> Woe to those who devise wickedness, and work evil upon their beds! When the morning dawns, they perform it, because it is in the power of their hand. They covet fields, and seize them; and houses, and take them away; they oppress a man and his house, a man and his inheritance. Therefore thus says the Lord: Behold, against this family I am devising evil, from which you cannot remove your necks; and you shall not walk haughtily, for it will be an evil time.
>
> *Micah 2:1–3*

> And I said: Hear, you heads of Jacob and rulers of the house of Israel! Is it not for you to know justice?—you who hate the good and love the evil, who tear the skin from off my people, and their flesh from off their bones . . . ?
>
> *Micah 3:1–2*

27

In our New Testament text we see the final form of cynicism which sees even God's presence as evil.

> As they were going away, behold, a dumb demoniac was brought to Jesus. And when the demon had been cast out, the dumb man spoke; and the crowds marveled, saying, "Never was anything like this seen in Israel." But the Pharisees said, "He casts out demons by the prince of demons."
>
> *Matthew 9:32–33*

Russell Baker, syndicated columnist, gave this year's commencement address at Connecticut College. He spoke of anger, and I want to borrow a few of his lines. "I grew up through the great depression," he said, "yet I have never seen a time when there were so many Americans so angry, or so mean spirited, or so sour about the country as they are today. Why has anger become the common response to the inevitable ups and downs of national life? The question is baffling not just because the American habit, even in the worst of times, has traditionally been mindless optimism, but also because there is so little for Americans to be angry about nowadays. We are the planet's one undisputed superpower. For the first time in sixty years, we enjoy something very much like real peace."[1] Note, too, the undisputed fact that we have more time for leisure, more gadgets to entertain us, and a longer, healthier life expectancy than any people since the dawn of history.

Yet everywhere anger seethes beneath the surface. I mean, it's gotten so bad a gentleman is afraid to open a door for a lady lest she call him a "sexist lout" and frame her comment in such profanity as would make a sailor blush. And if you're driving a little slowly, you dare not respond verbally to someone giving you the international gesture of contempt for fear he has a gun. A *Newsweek* poll finds that eighty-five percent of Americans feel there is less sense of community and fewer shared values than ever before.[2] Politicians, religious zealots, aggressive victims, and activists of every size and description exploit this mood and "flourish by sowing discontent. They triumph," says Baker, "by churning discontent into anger. Press, television, and radio also have a big financial stake in keeping the country boiling mad."[3] I would add that some churches thrive by keeping their members boiling mad at the latest enemy of God to be named by the minister.

From whence comes this anger? Politicians and religious zealots and card-carrying victims and activists and talk-show hosts have not created it. They simply fan it white hot and exploit it for their own purposes. What is the cause of this anger seething within us?

28

I want to suggest that the source of this anger is failed expectations—not simple, everyday expectations that we all need in order to keep going day after day, but expectations that are totally unrealistic to start with. These grandiose expectations must be perfectly fulfilled. No downsizing, no compromise will be tolerated, and they must be fulfilled quickly and easily, with no effort on our part. Of course the logical, reasonable thing to do when expectations fail is to draw back and look at them anew, perhaps trimming them down to fit reality. But that is the last thing we will do. Instead, we look for someone to blame for the failure; anyone but ourselves. Thus our seething anger.

Has the pursuit of unrealistic promises become the bricks and mortar of our way of life? Do we know of no way to present ourselves, our ideals, our products except by over-sell? What if the force that drives this relentless treadmill really is ever-new unrealistic promises stacked on the failed promises of yesterday?

This has profound theological significance. Does not all of this come from idolatry of self and from the insatiable wants of this self? My unrealistic expectations are expressions of what I demand for myself, and if I fancy myself to be a god, then obviously I deserve whatever I want. But when life fails and institutions fail and people fail, as they inevitably do, then I, the mighty sovereign of my tiny world, have been sinned against, and I am angry and unforgiving.

We self-ordained little gods are the very opposite of the one true God! When we fail him, he "is merciful and gracious, slow to anger and plenteous in mercy," but we, tin-pot gods that we are, are totally unforgiving.

Time was when people didn't expect life to be perfect; they accepted life's ups and downs as normal. Only in heaven would there be perfect justice and an end of suffering, pain, and disillusionment. But now we no longer believe in heaven. We expect heaven here and now, or at least a corner of paradise, when the children grow up and leave home and we can take early retirement. So when life fails and our hoped-for paradise turns out to be a little corner of hell, we are very angry. Our hopes and dreams have been foiled by someone: politicians, secular humanists, bumbling bureaucrats, the scientists who cut corners and turn in faulty research instead of finding solutions to all our problems, illegal immigrants, aliens from outer space. We must have someone to blame.

Time was when marriage was accepted as a very good but less-than-perfect institution. But now we expect marriage to be a sexual paradise, a mystical blending of two souls in perpetual bliss, the fulfillment of all our romantic fantasies, without any need for self-denial and pain. So marriage fails, as it always does, but instead of growing up a bit and humbling ourselves before reality, we seethe with anger, cast off the spouse who failed us, and go looking for someone who will know how blessed they are to have our divine affection bestowed upon them.

Time was when politics was accepted as a relative good. Folks had the good sense to know there are some things politicians can accomplish and other things that are totally beyond their reach. But now we expect government, whether on the national or local level, to end crime, hatch happy families, produce educated people, create loving neighbors, purify lust, even uphold faith in God. And when politics and politicians fail, we are outraged and cling to the illusion that all we need is to throw out the villains, elect new office holders, add new laws to the books, and Utopia will dawn eternal.

Time was when the church, the family, the legal profession, the medical profession, the military, the business world, colleges and universities—you name it—were all accepted as imperfect institutions that did many good things but were incapable of meeting everyone's needs. Only in heaven can all our needs be met, but even then, only after a radical conversion of our expectations. But that has all gone by the boards now. Sophisticated folks believe neither in God nor in heaven any more. Instead, we now expect perfection of everyone and everything, except, of course, of our own selves. We are infinitely forgiving of our own foibles, but infinitely unforgiving of other's. No wonder we are angry, mean-spirited, sour, and eager to believe the worst.

I said at the outset that anger can be constructive or destructive. I've already suggested one way in which our anger, stemming from failed expectations, could lead to something constructive. We could reevaluate our grandiose expectations and trim them to fit reality. A second thing: Our anger, redirected by God's grace, may just lead us to take a realistic look at ourselves. There's an outside possibility that I'm not as innocent and god-like as I need to think I am. I mean, if year after year, every relationship I enter into turns sour, maybe it's not that everyone else is a scoundrel, but that there is something sick in me that needs to be faced and cured. And now a third thing! Maybe, if our hearts can be gentled by the grace of God and our minds sharpened by a fierce integrity, we might just discover something good in those people and institutions that fail our bloated expectations.

Our failure to deal constructively with anger and our refusal to come to grips with the repeated failure of our idolatrous expectations leads to cynicism. And cynicism is the frigid, negative conviction that everyone and everything is totally bad, and that nothing is true or good or worthy of our devotion. Or to put it another way: Persistent anger is like living in

30

perpetual darkness. Eventually we're incapable of seeing light at all, though it is all around us. That is the curse of cynicism.

The response of certain Pharisees to Jesus' goodness shows the final form of cynicism. Angered by the obvious popularity and unmistakable goodness of this country rabbi with a Galilean accent and without a degree from any leading university, their jealous rage burned hotter and hotter until they were incapable of seeing anything good in him at all. "He casts out demons by the prince of demons," they said with an elitist sneer.

So the grace of God must gentle our anger lest cynicism destroy our very souls. Life does fail, but life is also good; infinitely good. So beware of smug cynics who see nothing about life worth loving and preserving, for if life itself is evil, then death is our greatest blessing and the sooner it comes, the better.

Marriage fails and wicked people do abuse and exploit their spouses, but marriage also offers the promise of lifelong love, forged out of the joys and tragedies which two weak human beings share together, by the grace of God. So beware the cynics who see nothing good in marriage and who build their reputations by condemning marriage. For if the bonding of two people in love is evil, then the isolated individual is the apex of human striving and loneliness is our greatest blessing.

Politicians fail and they are self-serving. Show me a human being who is not. But many politicians serve the public good and do it quite well, even those with whom we may disagree, though you'd never think it listening to the critics or to candidates running for office. Indeed, cynicism over politicians and government is more destructive of the common good than the worst things with which critics charge them, for cynicism cuts the vital nerve of the political will. Is this why so few vote?

In the present climate of failed expectations and anger it is easy to be cynical. And how superior we feel to be blessed with such wisdom and such moral insight as to detect the wrongs in everyone and everything. I mean, there are few more enlightened and superior human beings than ninth-grade girls at a slumber party who have suddenly discovered that their parents have feet of clay. But when adults, who should have learned a little humility and a little integrity along the way, persist in seeing only the failings of everyone and everything, when they delight in fomenting anger and mistrust, then the dark night of cynicism is fast falling and the light of goodness is fast becoming a forgotten dream.

The prayer printed at the top of today's order of worship is taken from our *Book of Common Worship*. It's entitled, "A Prayer for Joy in Others' Happiness."[4] We can and must, with equal fervor, pray for joy in others' goodness.

31

How desperately our world of angry people needs quiet agents of God's grace who will <u>rejoice in the goodness of others.</u> And whom can God count on for such simple miracles but modest Christians like some of you, whose greatest honor is to follow and serve Jesus Christ who "went about doing good and healing all who were oppressed?"[5] Remember then whom we serve and who we are!

5

"No One Comes to the Father But by Me"

John 14:1–7

RECENTLY I TAUGHT OUR JOHN KNOX BIBLE CLASS. THE lesson was on the fourteenth chapter of John. Afterwards a very dear and special friend suggested that I put part of that lesson into a sermon. And since the material was still fresh and had been helpful to her, I decided to take her good advice.

Let me mention one other reason. Recently the Session read a scholarly article which attempts to explain why so many young adults who grew up in the Presbyterian Faith have left the church. One disturbing answer: They never learned what makes Christianity distinctive; they were starved theologically. In their minds, Christianity is simply about ethics and thus is no different from any other religion with high moral values.

Well, you can't encounter the fourteenth chapter of John without discovering there is something disturbingly unique about this Jesus.

As I read the lesson, I want you to listen as if you are hearing this word of God for the first time. It won't be easy. This scripture is read at almost every funeral service you've ever attended, so you almost know it by heart. And knowing it by heart, you're sure you already know what it means. So your ears are stopped and your hearts closed to the creative word of God that is always fresh and new. Will you scrub your mind of all assumptions and struggle to hear this word of God as if hearing it for the very first time?

Jesus said to his grieving disciples: "Let not your hearts be troubled; believe in God, believe also in me. In my Father's house are many rooms; if it were not so, would I have told you that I go to prepare a place for you? And when I go and prepare a place for you, I will come again and will take you to myself, that where I am you may be also. And you know the way where I am going. Thomas said to him, "Lord, we do not know where you are going; how can we know the way?" Jesus said to him, "I am the way, and the truth, and the life; no one comes to the Father but by me. If you had known me, you would have known my Father also; henceforth you know him and have seen him."

John 14:1–7

I'm sure I've been in on a hundred and one bull sessions when the topic was, "Who will be saved?" You know how the discussion goes. Someone says, "I can't believe that people are doomed to hell just because they don't believe in Jesus. What about the poor woman in darkest Africa who dies never having heard of Jesus Christ or the gentle Buddhist monk who is more Christ-like than a lot of Christians? I can't believe God would be so unfair as to damn them." Someone else chimes in, "But that's what the Bible teaches. Didn't Jesus Himself say, 'I am the way, and the truth, and the life; no one comes to the Father but by me.'?"

I suppose this verse is used more than any other in the Bible as an alleged proof that only believing Christians will be saved. And what I want to say is that this verse has little to do with this particular question. If it did, I would argue that "salvation" has a particularly Christian meaning which sets it apart from all other salvic hopes. For example, "Nirvana," the salvic goal for Buddhists and "Paradise," the salvic goal for Muslims, are both something quite different from the Christian hope of salvation. Accordingly, Buddha could well have said that he is the only way to Nirvana, and Mohammed, that he is the only way to Paradise.[1] But instead of salvation, Jesus had something quite different in mind. The sermon this morning explores this difference.

Let me begin by pointing out what Jesus did not say. He did not say, "No one comes to God but by me!" Instead he said, "No one comes to the Father but by me!" An insignificant matter of words? Anyone who has drawn up a will or proposed marriage or received a medical diagnosis knows that words have precise meanings which are terribly important, especially where God is concerned. And no one was more precise than Jesus in choosing words to express the reality that mattered most to him. So I want to suggest that a proper understanding of this verse and of the entire fourteenth chapter of John hinges on Jesus' use of "Father" rather than "God."

In the gospel according to John, the name "God" occurs fifty-six times by my count, but "Father" occurs one hundred and twenty-one times. Why this disparity? Obviously "Father" meant for Jesus a reality that could not be expressed by the name "God" alone.

Now consider another remarkable fact. Jesus did not speak of "His Father" in public, but only to His intimate friends. This is all the more

34

remarkable when you consider that in the first century everyone spoke of God as Father. Every little god of every pagan nation was called "Father." And in Israel, prophets and psalmists and sages had spoken of God as Father for centuries. So Jesus was not presenting a new, revolutionary idea.

Yet in Matthew, Mark, and Luke, Jesus almost never speaks in public of his Father in heaven. "Why this extraordinary reserve on the part of Jesus in speaking about what was a theological commonplace? The question practically answers itself. The fatherhood of God was not a theological commonplace for Jesus."[2] When he did speak of the fatherhood of God, he did it privately and only to his closest friends and followers. And then only after a very significant event had occurred.

If you've studied the gospels you know that a sharp dividing line runs across Jesus' public ministry. After a popular public ministry in Galilee, Jesus withdrew and was alone praying. His disciples gathered around him. For all his popularity with the crowds, they didn't have the slightest idea who he was or what he was about. So he said to his disciples, "You've been with me for some time now, do you have any inkling of who I am?" Peter said, "You are the Christ, the promised Messiah." But instead of telling his disciples to make it known far and wide, he charged them to tell no one.[3]

It's also interesting that after this Jesus had less and less to say to the multitudes. Instead, he concentrated on his intimate friends, on those blessed few who couldn't possibly leave him because they somehow sensed that in Jesus they were in touch with a spiritual reality of extraordinary intensity. So it was only to them, after Peter's confession, that he spoke increasingly of God as "my Father" and "your Father." Was the relationship Jesus shared with his Father of such meaning that it could only be shared, if at all, with this noble, blessed few who had left everything to follow him, who understood something of the deepest secrets of his heart, and who thus knew to remove their shoes and bow their heads before this holy of holies?

Maybe you've had an experience so moving and so personal that you could only speak of it to one or two loved ones, to those few who respect the heights and depths your soul can reach, those whom you can trust with the deepest secrets of your heart. If so, then you can begin to understand, however faintly, why Jesus could share the unique relationship he had with his Father only with these few who loved him.

And how was it that Jesus knew the Father as no one else? It was because his greatest joy and greatest purpose was to do his Father's will, even unto death. He was the Son of the Father who was truly obedient, the son Israel had failed to be, so he could say, "He that has seen me has seen the Father."[4] And if you ask what it was about this Jesus that made him so obedient, that so set him free from self that he could delight in doing his Father's will as no one else before or since, you have asked the very question with which the church has always wrestled in trying to define the incomprehensible greatness of Jesus Christ.

I remember reading somewhere that if it takes genius to write magnificent music, it takes equal genius to interpret and perform the music as the composer intended. That can occur only if the performer is able to capture the mind and heart of the composer. There are many who can play the right notes, even play them perfectly, but they are not one with the composer. Only rarely does a performer come along who so enters into the heart and mind of the composer, who is so obedient, if I can use that word, that when he plays you can almost say that the spirit of the composer is incarnate in him.

In 1954, Van Cliburn won the Tchaikovsky competition in Moscow. He was the first non-Russian ever to win that award. He played Peter Ilyich Tchaikovsky's "Concerto in B-Flat Minor, No. 1" perhaps as no one had played it since the composer himself. In that sense it could be said that if you wanted to know Tchaikovsky, you could know him only through Van Cliburn in Moscow in the month of June, 1954.

Jesus' oneness with God the Father was unique. It was so profound, intimate, and unsearchable, in fact, that he could say, "No one comes to the Father but by me." God may have given to others secrets about his nature and purpose: Moses, Isaiah, John the Baptist. And I am willing to include Socrates, Mohammed, and Buddha in this illustrious group, but when it comes to knowing as Father the hidden and incomprehensible mystery we call God, no one is on the field but this Jesus, son of Mary, who was crucified, dead and buried, and was raised on the third day as the promise of our poor lives. He and the Father were one as no one else before or since.

One other point must be made. Who was qualified to say that Van Cliburn was the way to Peter Ilyich Tchaikovsky? Not you and I, and not your typical disk jockey; only serious musicians who know and love great music enough to be able to recognize genius when it comes along.

And what is more, only those who have been with Jesus, like the disciples and maybe some of us, who have begun to comprehend something of the mystery that Jesus is, and who have learned from him that God the Father is the ultimate joy—we alone can have a hint of what it meant to Jesus Christ to love and be loved by the Father. And we alone are qualified, if any one is qualified, to know if Jesus Christ is the way to the Father, not those proud of heart and mind who've never given themselves to him, but the meek and lowly of heart who have found in this Jesus a promise and a glory that not even death can silence. Have you known it, this promise and glory?

We began with talk about bull sessions discussing who will be saved. Do you still think this is what Jesus' gracious words are all about? I hope not, because if you do, your ears are still stopped and your heart still closed to this word of God.

One of the great sins of religion is to take God's word of grace and change it into a law that puts a spiritual crevice between people, to take his offer of love and intimacy to us, and to use it for the damnation of others.[5]

Who will be saved? Only God is qualified to make that decision, and knowing what we know of the Father in and through Jesus Christ, we can be assured that he is equal to that task. And we? It is our calling to accept Jesus' invitation to the glory and love of the Father and to give ourselves to this greatest adventure of the soul, an adventure that knows no end. Then we will have something to tell others that may awaken their hidden longing for the God and Father of us all. And we'll not be bothered with the academic question: "Who will and who won't be saved?"

In the first chapter of John's account of the gospel, Philip meets Jesus and knows somehow that he is in the presence of ultimate mystery. Philip then goes to his brother Nathanel and says simply, "Come and see." We can do no more. But first we must have found and seen and known a hint of the Father's love in this Jesus. Have you? If not, then Jesus Christ will remain for you an enigma, for "the love of Jesus, what it is, only His loved ones know."[6]

37

6

On Being Responsible for
Our Lives

Genesis 3:8–13; John 5:39–40, 45–47

BEFORE READING THE SCRIPTURE LESSONS FOR THE morning, let me tell a little story that may give you some idea where I'm headed. Twenty-three years ago when I was the new preacher, I was standing back there at the Tower Exit to speak to people after worship. One lady shook my hand, thanked me for the sermon, and then proceeded to fall down the steps. Several of us rushed to her aid and got her on her feet. Fortunately the only thing hurt was her pride. In her total embarrassment she blurted out that I was to blame for her fall. "You don't stand where Dr. Hollingsworth used to stand," said she.

The question is this: Why are we always quick to accuse or to blame another when things go wrong in our lives? And where do you draw the line between one person's involvement and another person's responsibility? I was standing at a different spot. Keep this in mind as I read our two scriptures, one from the Book of Genesis, the other from the gospel According to John.

> And (Adam and Eve) heard the sound of the Lord God walking in the garden in the cool of the day, and the man and his wife hid themselves from the presence of the Lord God among the trees of the garden. But the Lord God called to the man, and said to him, "Where are you?" And he said, "I heard the sound of thee in the garden, and I was afraid, because I was naked; and I hid myself." He said, "Who told you that you were naked? Have you eaten of the tree of which I commanded you not to eat?" The man said, "The woman thou gavest to be with me, she gave me fruit of the tree, and I ate." Then the Lord God said to the woman, "What is this that you have done?" The woman said, "The serpent beguiled me, and I ate."
>
> *Genesis 3:8–13*

Jesus said, You search the scriptures, because you think that in them you have eternal life; and it is they that bear witness to me; yet you refuse to come to me that you may have life. . . . Do not think that I shall accuse you to the Father; it is Moses who accuses you, on whom you set your hope. If you believed Moses, you would believe me, for he wrote of me. But if you do not believe his writings, how will you believe my words?

John 5:39–40, 45–47

Where do you draw the line between your responsibility for your own life and the responsibility of others who influence your life? Another question! Does the fact that we believe in Jesus Christ make a difference in the way we draw this line?

Let me bring the issue into focus with a story. It is not a true story. It is a parable of blame and the complacency of self that speaks of the sinfulness in all of us.

A young woman reached the end of her rope and went to a counselor for help. She was twenty-nine years of age, and the story she told was of one failure after another. In high school she'd not only been an excellent student, she'd also been popular enough and vivacious enough to be head cheer leader. But in college her life began to unravel. Her grades were barely good enough to qualify for graduation, and in the eight years since graduation she'd gone through two nasty divorces and several unhappy jobs. And she was estranged from her family.

In her second session with the counselor, she was asked to tell about her parents and her early family life. Doesn't every counselor who has read Sigmund Freud believe that's the source of all personal problems? It was a typical story: a good middle-class family that went to church together and vacationed together. Her father was a successful businessman; he was also scoutmaster for a Boy Scout troop at the church. Her mother was a traditional wife and mother who prided herself in providing a warm and loving home, and she chaired the committee for volunteers at one of the local hospitals. Her older brother was a successful lawyer, happily married with two children. Her younger sister was married to a minister; they had one child with a second one on the way.

She said there had been normal arguments and disagreements, but by and large it had been a loving and happy home. However, she did resent the fact that her parents expected the three of them to go to church with them and to share in keeping the house clean and neat. She also resented that her

39

parents expected the three of them to have summer jobs to earn some of their own spending money. But worst of all, she felt no one in her family understood her, and the fact that they were all successful and had their lives together put undue pressure on her to do something with her life when she didn't feel like doing anything special. So she'd convinced herself that their success and their happiness and their values were to blame for her misery. Clearly anything wrong with her life was their fault, not her's.

Anna Russell captured this petulant, narcissistic spirit in a little rhyme.

> At three I had a feeling of
> Ambivalence toward my brothers,
> And so it follows naturally
> I poisoned all my lovers.
> But now I'm happy; I have learned
> The lesson this has taught;
> That everything I do that's wrong
> Is someone else's fault.[1]

Fortunately, her counselor refused to let her wiggle out of facing up to her own responsibility for her life. This was not easy for her to do; it was the hardest thing she'd ever had to do. Encouraged by a culture always on the hunt for someone to blame, she had fallen for the popular fallacy of mistaking influences for causes, as if her family had made her the way she was and as if she had no responsibility for her own response or reaction to those influences. But gradually, over a period of weeks, her counselor led her to see that she had primary responsibility for the mess she had made of her life and that there was not much hope for life getting better until she accepted that responsibility. Her counselor did one more thing: He helped her understand that there are no perfect families, that her's was far, far better than most, and that they needed her acceptance and love every bit as much as she needed theirs.

Unfortunately, too few stories end like this. It is a truism that other people influence our lives, and some influences are better than others. In fact, some influences are so destructive you marvel that anyone survives, emotionally or physically. The influences they exert upon our lives are their responsibility, not ours. But the way we deal with them and interpret them, whether we let them consume us with resentment, self-pity, arrogance, and laziness, or whether we let them fill us with gratitude and determination is no one's responsibility but our own. And wisdom belongs to those who know the difference.

40

On Being Responsible for Our Lives

Too many don't know the difference and go through life blaming others, especially their families, for what they themselves have done with their lives. And what is more, too many counselors and would-be helpers don't seem to know the difference either. During forty-one years of ministry, I have seen too many heartbroken parents who have been rejected by children who blame them for the unhappiness in their lives. The story is often the same: The child had trouble adjusting to life, went to counselors or to sympathetic friends, and from what they heard, concluded that their parents were to blame for their unhappy lives.

This is an attitude all too common today. Children blame parents for all their problems; the divorced blame their former spouses for whatever went wrong. If Junior can't learn, it's always the teacher's fault; if I can't hold a job, it's always the company's fault; if society is falling apart, it's always the government's fault; if religion doesn't satisfy my needs, it's always the church's fault or the preacher's fault. The last thing we will do is accept responsibility for what we do with our lives. And how interesting it is that if life goes well and our efforts are crowned with success, we are quick to take full credit for that. But if life turns sour, we are just as quick to blame everyone but ourselves.

When God found Adam hiding in the garden, He asked why he had eaten the forbidden fruit. "The woman you gave me, caused me to eat." Was Adam trying to shift the blame not only on Eve but on God as well? And when God confronted Eve, she said, "The serpent beguiled me and I ate." It's the serpent's fault, not mine. But God held Adam and Eve and the serpent responsible for their particular part in that ancient tragedy.

God did one more thing that often escapes our notice. He did not deny that he'd given the women to Adam, nor did he argue the fact that Eve and the serpent had a part in this oldest of all tragedies. Nor did he wash his hands of these creatures he had made who now possessed the power to break his heart. Instead, he loved them, even in their ruin and shame and guilt—so much, in fact, that in the fulness of time he sent his only begotten Son to share our human lot and set us free from sin and death. We who would like to be gods, and find it difficult to admit the impossibility, are we, or are any of the gods of this world, willing to accept the incomprehensible responsibility that was and is God's?

Maybe you have borne a burden of blame from someone you love. And maybe, even though love remains for that one who has shifted all the guilt upon you, the burden gets heavier and heavier each year. One of the hardest things we will ever have to do is to go on loving and praying for those who falsely blame us for their lives. And that only adds to the burden we already

41

carry in our concern for that person's pain. But to be blamed for the pain is almost too much.

There is no easy solution. There are no magic words that will take away the burden you feel. But never forget that the God who loves you carries that burden with you. Does that make it easier to bear?

Remember the words of our Lord! "Come to me, all who labor and are heavy laden, and I will give you rest. Take my yoke upon you, and learn from me; for I am gentle and lowly in heart, and you will find rest for your souls. For my yoke is easy, and my burden is light."[2]

7

Life Can Begin Again

Luke 19:1–10

I HAVE CHOSEN FOR OUR TEXT THE FAMILIAR STORY OF Zacchaeus. You'll find it at the beginning of the nineteenth chapter of Luke. Incidentally, this chapter ends with Jesus' entry into Jerusalem on what we call "Palm Sunday." So Jesus' encounter with Zacchaeus must have something to do with Palm Sunday and the events that follow in Jerusalem. But what? I want to suggest that in Luke's mind the story of Zacchaeus is symbolic of the power of Jesus to change human life, even the life of a disgraced and despised rich man. If Zacchaeus can be changed by the word of Jesus, how much more the crucified and risen Lord can change us poor mortals! Do you believe your life can be different? Hear again how life began anew for Zacchaeus!

> He entered Jericho and was passing through. And there was a man named Zacchaeus; he was a chief tax collector, and rich. And he sought to see who Jesus was, but could not, on account of the crowd, because he was small of stature. So he ran on ahead and climbed up into a sycamore tree to see him, for he was to pass that way. And when Jesus came to the place, he looked up and said to him, "Zacchaeus, make haste and come down; for I must stay at your house today." So he made haste and came down, and received him joyfully. And when they saw it they all murmured, "He has gone in to be the guest of a man who is a sinner." And Zacchaeus stood and said to the Lord, "Behold, Lord, the half of my goods I give to the poor; and if I have defrauded any one of anything, I restore it fourfold." And Jesus said to him, "Today salvation has come to this house, since he also is a son of Abraham. For the Son of man came to seek and to save the lost."
>
> *Luke 19:1–10*

The New Testament stands on the conviction that the gospel can change lives. Every page assumes that Jesus Christ can make us new and different people. Do we still believe it's possible? I read an interesting comment the other day. The writer, a theologian in one of our seminaries, said that in some churches there is far more optimism about the possibility of changing society than there is about changing the lives of individuals. "Yet it is just this hope that human life, the concrete life of individuals, can be transformed and moved from darkness to light that is the consistent message of the New Testament."[1] Do we believe we can become different persons? A more searching question: Do we want to become different persons?

In his book, *Life Can Begin Again*, Helmut Thielicke says that we in the modern world are in the grip of two fears that negate the hope of changing our lives: fear of the past and fear of the future.

We are afraid the past will never allow us to be different. On the one hand, history molds the present, severely limiting our options. For example, none of us brought slaves to America, but we are all victims of that dreadful historic crime and it sets the agenda of so much that we do. On the other hand, consider the history of our individual lives. The millions of people who seek psychiatric help give grim evidence of the common desire to be free of an individual past that holds us in its iron grip. There is not one among us whose life is not in bondage to something in the past we would give anything to undo: the influence of an abusive or an unwise person who twisted our lives; a teenage mistake that left deep, indelible scars; a hasty decision that sent us down an irreversible path. And whatever we do, whether we're conscious of it or not, the heavy hand of that past holds us mercilessly in its grip.

But if we are not free of the past, neither are we free of the future that looms so ominously ahead of us. For all the optimistic rhetoric of our leaders, we know in our bones that the spread of atomic weapons and rampant population growth and the destruction of our environment are beyond our control. And anyone who thinks we control the future is living in a world of illusions. More than this, the fear of vegetating in some nursing home casts a dark shadow over the present, reminding us of the dark side of medical progress. And the healthier we live as we advance in years, the more we increase our chances of ending up in a nursing home. And beyond that, death mocks all our values. The future, no less than the past, holds us in its iron grip and dictates so much of what we can and want to do.

We know we can't undo the past. We also know we can neither escape the future nor control it. And yet we go on believing we can be different. But how? "What we need and what we yearn for," says Thielicke, "is something that will liberate us from paralysis and help us gain a new attitude toward what lies behind us and ahead of us."[2]

With this in mind I want to go back to Zacchaeus, that little man whose life was so radically changed. Who knows, perhaps we'll discover things we failed to see when we first read of his encounter with Jesus.

The first thing that strikes me is that Zacchaeus didn't go looking for Jesus in order to get his life changed. I simply can't imagine Zacchaeus sitting at the breakfast table with his coffee and morning paper, reading that Jesus was coming to town and saying to himself, "Let me see, being so short I've got this inferiority complex that keeps me from making friends" or "I feel guilty about my line of work, I sure could use a more positive attitude when I go out there to raise tax money! By George, I think I'll have my shower and get dressed and pay a visit to this traveling miracle worker to see if he can straighten out the kinks in my life!"

It was nothing like that. Zacchaeus simply wanted to see this Jesus of Nazareth about whom everyone was talking; this Jesus whom everyone said was saying something fresh and new about God. I'll grant that he may have been unhappy with himself; who isn't? I'll also grant that he went to see Jesus in hopes he'd hear some word of inspiration that would keep him going a little longer. But he didn't go to Jesus with a list of problems he wanted solved in order to improve his life. If that had been his intention, I can assure you he would have found Jesus profoundly disappointing, just as some of us do who give Jesus a try, expecting him to solve our problems.

So what was it that changed Zacchaeus' life? To ask this question is to ask what kind of change Jesus Christ brings to pass in our lives. It is a change at the very center of our lives, a change that replaces an inordinate love of self with a new love for God so we can be free to love ourselves and others with creative love.

Most of us, when we think about changing our lives, think it can be accomplished by greater effort on our part. "I want to quit over-indulging at the dinner table, or I want to begin exercising, or I want to concentrate harder on being nice to other people, or I want to know how to study so I can make better grades. Where can I go to find help in achieving these good things? Maybe I'll try Jesus to see if he can give me a boost. I may even join the church to see if that will help."

More often than not I quit trying and end up feeling guilty. But if I'm successful, you know exactly what happens. I hold my head high and look down my pious nose at all those poor under-achievers who could be just as perfect as I if they only tried harder. And lo and behold, another self-righteous Pharisee stinks up the church, and I am no closer to the kingdom of God than I was when I began my regimen of self-improvement. Indeed, I am farther from that kingdom, because the malignant self-love at the core of my being has put down stronger and deeper roots into my soul.

This is not to say that such efforts to change our behavior are unimportant. They are. But such changes in our behavior do not go to the root of our trouble. Our fundamental trouble is that we are "ego-centered" when we are created to be "God-centered." We judge "everything by the way it affects the ego: myself, my race, my family, my church, my country."[3] No, our greatest need is to be saved from our own selves. And that is not done by trying harder to change ourselves nor by using the inspiration of Jesus to effect the changes we want for ourselves. That only increases our bondage to self. No, it is done when we find in him one so good and so perfect that he awakens the best hopes we have within us, and, without knowing quite what is happening, we suddenly love him and God-in-him so deeply we forget ourselves altogether. And from that moment on our deepest intention is not to please ourselves but the one who has called us from death into life. This is what happened to Zacchaeus when Jesus Christ entered his life.

It is the same thing that happens to every humble Christian who finds in Christ a new beginning. No longer does fear or guilt or hostility from the past dictate our response to life, for our past has been forgiven. No longer does fear of the future dictate our response to life, for in Jesus Christ we have found him who is coming to meet us from the *eschaton*, the God-intended end of all things. Because of him everything now is different.

If this sounds strange to you, I can only say I'm sorry you've not yet known what it is to love and to be loved by the Savior of us all. "The love of Jesus, what it is; none but His loved ones know."[4] But you will know in due time. This is what God created you for.

Let me cite briefly one other thing I see in this story of Zacchaeus!

Aren't you a little surprised that Jesus said nothing to Zacchaeus about the evil of his ways? He simply loved him and asked him if he could come into the house of his life. I can assure you, had I been the prophet of righteousness who confronted Zacchaeus, instead of Jesus, the approach would have been different. I'd have climbed up into my high moral pulpit and reminded old Zacchaeus that he was exploiting the poor people of Jericho in violation of God's will. Isn't this the way Amos would have done it, or any modern prophet of righteousness who has had a taste of liberation theology? And if I'd been successful as a prophet of righteousness and if Zacchaeus had been a man who still had a conscience, I might have made him feel guilty enough to go a little easier with the poor people of Jericho. But I would not have touched those dark places of the soul where only the love of God can change unconcern into love, darkness into light, and death into life.

Is this why we change so little? Is it because we and the church know how to dispense guilt but not forgiveness, how to create fear but not hope, how to inspire hostility but not love, how to encourage death but not life?

But I suspect there's a far deeper reason why we change so little. It's because we really do not want to be different. Why should we? We've got everything we need: food and shelter and money and endless forms of diversion and recreation to escape from ourselves. And, if we occasionally get depressed, all sorts of "spiritual" help is available to reinforce our complacency and self-esteem. We have everything we need except a heart that's alive to God. And I have discovered that even when life turns sour and nothing turns out as we'd hoped, that even if life becomes a living hell, we would rather endure that hell than admit there's anything in us that needs to be changed.

Does not W. H. Auden's poem, "The Age of Anxiety" speak of this intransigence in all of us?

> . . . it is silly
> To refuse the tasks of time.
> And, overlooking our lives,
> Cry—"Miserable wicked me,
> How interesting I am."
> We would rather be ruined than changed,
> We would rather die in our dread
> Than climb the cross of the moment
> And let our illusions die.[5]

So I suspect it really comes down to this: Do I want to be changed so life can begin again? If we ever come to this decision—and God will pursue us and disturb us even in death to make us face up to it—we will make it because our eyes are opened to the dreadful love of God that wraps our pitiful little lives in a hope greater than death. And when we want our eyes to be opened to this love and this hope, so great will be our joy that nothing will be able to keep us from becoming true children of God. And then, what we say and do and dream for ourselves and others will reflect the goodness of Jesus Christ who loved us and gave himself for us.

8

Three Popular
Misunderstandings of Faith

Philippians 3:12–21

ABOUT TWENTY YEARS AGO I GAVE UP GOLF. IT WAS taxing what little religion I had. I had this slice that sent a ball soaring like a boomerang. Every time I addressed the ball, it was going to be like smashing a soft ball over the center field fence. I'd try to correct it and hook the ball far to the left. So I quit. I was spending all my time looking for balls. The root of my problem was that I didn't have any lessons when I took up the game, just a few pointers from a pal who had become an expert watching his daddy play. Years later, when I tried a couple of lessons from Ross Taylor, the Pro in Black Mountain, North Carolina, I didn't try hard enough to unlearn my bad habits.

The learning process, whether it has to do with golf, speaking proper English, or growing in the Christian faith, not only requires a desire to learn new things but also a willingness to unlearn old things. The sermon this morning is about three popular misunderstandings of the faith we must unlearn if we hope to become mature Christians whom God and the world can count on. Our text for the morning is about Paul's quest for the high calling of Jesus Christ.

> Not that I have already obtained this or am already perfect; but I press on to make it my own, because Christ Jesus has made me his own. Brethren, I do not consider that I have made it my own; but one thing I do, forgetting what lies behind and straining forward to what lies ahead, I press on toward the goal for the prize of the upward call of God in Christ Jesus. Let those of us who are mature be thus minded; and if in anything you are otherwise minded, God will reveal that also to you. Only let us hold true to what we have attained.

> Brethren, join in imitating me, and mark those who so live as you have an example in us. For many, of whom I have often told you and now tell

you even with tears, live as enemies of the cross of Christ. Their end is destruction, their god is the belly, and they glory in their shame, with minds set on earthly things. But our commonwealth is in heaven, and from it we await a Savior, the Lord Jesus Christ, who will change our lowly body to be like his glorious body, by the power that enables him even to subject all things to himself.

Philippians 3:12–21

The end of all our growing and living is to know Jesus Christ our Lord. But how do we grow in this knowledge, this faith, this love? In answering this question it is absolutely essential to know that our relationship with Jesus Christ is deepened, not as a result of our concentrated efforts, but of his quiet, transforming friendship for us. And our hardest task is to get our selves out of the way so there can be an open space in the center of our lives which he can occupy and recreate.

A minister of the Dutch Reformed Church tells of a visit from Mario Cuomo, governor of New York. The governor had spoken in his church on Thanksgiving. The governor surveyed the books in his study, and then said, "Have you heard W. H. Auden's comment that a real book reads us? Which of these books have read you?"[1] Some of you know what he meant. Seminal books, the kind of books you treasure and reread again and again, possess us and change our lives. It is not so much that we master them; it's as if the author's vision comes through the words and masters us.

It's like this with artists, I am told. The artist's greatest task is to get herself out of the way, to quit trying to control the creative moment, so the object, the vision, can enter her and paint through her. In the same way I have discovered that my best writing occurs in those rare moments when I can forget myself altogether and let the mystery of words write through me. I take it that Paul knew exactly what this means. "I count everything as loss because of the surpassing worth of knowing Christ Jesus my Lord. For his sake I have suffered the loss of all things, and count them as refuse, in order that I may gain Christ and be found in him, not having a righteousness of my own, based on law, but that which is through faith in Christ. . . . "

"Righteousness that is through the law" is one's own achievement; it creates people who are harsh and self-righteous. It's like the books we read, the pictures we paint, the words we write. But righteousness that is through faith in Christ is a gift that fills us with joy and self-forgetfulness, like the books that read us, the visions that paint us, the words that write us. The greatest things in life are always gifts of grace that come to us in spite of the worst we are and of the best we are.

49

With this in mind, let me cite three misunderstandings that inhibit Christ's possession of us.

The first is the mistaken belief that a conversion experience is the sole requirement for being a Christian. There are some who believe that once you've accepted Jesus there's nothing more you need to do. For such people the main reason for going to church is to have a dramatic conversion experience, or, if they've already been "saved," to share vicariously the emotions of new converts.

It is not my purpose to deny the need for a radical decision of faith. The decision to follow Jesus Christ demands of all of us a sharp break with our own sinful past and with the sinful ways of the world. And it may well be that we Presbyterian-types don't make enough of the need for a clear-cut decision of faith. Nonetheless, there are at least two things wrong with this popular belief that conversion is the whole of being a Christian.

First, people of this persuasion often insist that there's only one kind of valid conversion experience: a dramatic, emotional upheaval that takes you down the aisle as the choir sings, "Just as I Am, Without One Plea." How can that be when no two people are exactly alike, and when each person has his or her own special way of answering the call of Christ? What is important is not the kind of experience but the sincerity with which we say, "Lord Jesus, from this moment on my life belongs to you!"

Second, conversion is but the beginning of faith. It's like marriage. Marriage is meant to be the beginning of a lifelong relationship that keeps drawing us out of our little private shells so we can share life with another. And you don't have to be a genius to know that any couple whose idea of marriage never grows beyond the emotional level of wedding and honeymoon is doomed to failure. In the same way, you're born to begin the adventure of life, and you're born again to begin the greater adventure of eternal life. Christians who want only the experience of being born again over and over again are like Peter Pan who flees the world of adult responsibilities for the fantasies of childhood.

Conversion is not the whole of Christianity, only the first step in a life-long process of being recreated by the grace of God. And I have found that people who cling to a conversion experience as their claim on salvation are often the least able to open their frightened little lives to Jesus Christ so he can read them and paint them and write them into his likeness. This misunderstanding we must unlearn.

The second misunderstanding that is widely held is that the purpose of Christianity is to make us good. In the minds of many, the church is the guardian of public morals and fulfills its purpose when it teaches us to be good, law-abiding citizens. More than once during my childhood my parents and teachers used God as a threat to try to make me behave. "If you're a bad boy God will be angry with you." When my mother was particularly frustrated by my antics and she couldn't keep her eye on me, she relied on God to be some sort of moral baby-sitter to keep me in line.

We smile, but many of us operate on the same assumption. If we're Christian teachers who fancy ourselves the divinely appointed guardians of morality, how often we come down on our students, whether children or adults, with the grim reminder that Christians are to be morally superior. In fact, you've heard such words from this Teaching Elder. And doesn't the unbelieving world often condemn the church precisely because Christians are not better than they are? Indeed, don't you often hear the comment that you don't have to be a Christian to be honest and chaste and loving? And those who ask are exactly right. You don't have to be a Christian in order to be morally upright. There are countless Jews and Buddhists and Moslems and Hindus and atheists who are morally superior to most of us.

Christianity is not an ethical system nor is the church the divinely appointed teacher of morality. Christianity is the joyful celebration of God's gracious and unrelenting work to restore us and the whole of creation to our rightful destiny. The gospel is the proclamation of God's forgiveness in Jesus Christ, not an onerous challenge to try harder to obey the moral law. Or as Helmut Thielicke once put it: "People think the purpose of the gospel is only to make people better, more serious, more respectable, when its real purpose is rather that death may be conquered"[2]—the death of the spirit that comes upon us when, in dreadful moments of existential honesty, we see how wicked we really are and we sink into despair; the death that swallows us up when everything fails: our health, our career, our family and friends, our dreams, and life no longer has meaning, and we are tempted to give up. That's the purpose of the gospel: to set our weak lives on the firm foundation of God's love so we won't give up or quit, but keep prying open the heavy door to our hearts so Jesus Christ can come in, when it would be so much easier to give in to defeat and death.

And yet faith in Jesus Christ does make us better. But there is a wide gulf between those who achieve their moral stature through rigorous self-denial, through obeying the moral law even when they find it odious, and those who allow the grace of God to gentle and better their lives. The moral achievements of the one results in the self-righteous Pharisee of the New Testament and the modern world who is haughty, abrasive, judgmental, unbending. The morality of the other, having been read and painted and written into their lives by the grace of Christ, makes them joyful, humble, loving, and a

51

delight to be around. And it is worth noting that Jesus' harshest words were not directed at sinners who gave in to the sins of the flesh, the kinds of sins that make the news and horrify the righteous defenders of morality. No, his most biting words were directed precisely at the righteous whose pride in their moral achievements made them the kind of friendless, joyless people others try to avoid. This misunderstanding we must unlearn.

The third misunderstanding that keeps us from being mature Christians is the belief that faith will protect us from hardship and suffering. There are plenty of false prophets who spread this lie, and plenty of gullible people eager to believe it. "Put your faith in Jesus," we're told, "and God will give you an enchanting love life, multiply your investments, protect you from arthritis, keep calamities from your door, and generally bless you with unmitigated happiness. And on top of this he will throw in heaven as an added reward."

Not only are such false promises a direct contradiction of the Christian faith, not only are people who buy into such promises doomed to disillusionment, but such belief makes us worse sinners. If worship of self and the things that enhance such idolatrous worship are a major part of our basic sinfulness, and if growing in our relationship with Jesus Christ requires getting ourselves and our self-centered desires out of the way, then such belief drives us farther from the true God.

Some weeks ago I picked up a little book in my library. It had been waiting a long time to be read. *Creative Suffering, the Ripple of Hope*, is its title. One of its contributors, a wise shepherd of souls, writes about this struggle to put our idolatrous self aside so Christ can nurture our true and better self. "Only in our voluntarily dying to ourselves in the aloneness of our own spirit can God live in us. The greatest suffering is, therefore, not of the body but of the spirit. . . . There is always the pain of separating from certain narrower, less generous forms of living and reaching upward to identify with one's higher self."[3]

The belief that the purpose of our faith is to protect us from hardship and suffering is wrong. Faith in Jesus Christ is a summons to a rigorous struggle, especially with our own sinful selves. So if, in your heart and mind, there are any traces of this false belief, then shed it like the deadly plague that it is so Jesus Christ can read you and paint you and write you into his likeness.

9

Who Needs a Savior?

1 Timothy 1:12–17

TILL THE END OF HIS LIFE THE APOSTLE PAUL NEVER ceased to marvel that Christ Jesus had entrusted such a man as he with the gospel of God's love and forgiveness. After all, he had mercilessly persecuted Jesus' followers. So it was not unusual for him to break forth into adulations of joy that Christ had chosen him to be an apostle. Our text for the morning is one such instance.

> I thank him who has made me equal to the task, Christ Jesus our Lord; I thank him for judging me worthy of this trust and appointing me to his service—even though I used to be a blasphemer and did all I could to injure and discredit the faith. But because I acted ignorantly in unbelief I was dealt with mercifully; the grace of our Lord was lavished upon me, with the faith and love which are ours in Christ Jesus. Here are words you may trust, words that nobody should doubt: "Christ Jesus came into the world to save sinners"; I myself being the greatest of them. And if mercy has been shown to me, it is because Jesus Christ meant to make me the greatest evidence of his inexhaustible patience for all the other people who would later have to trust in him to come to eternal life. Now to the King of all worlds, immortal, invisible, the only God, be honor and glory for ever and ever! Amen. (This translation blends wording from the New English Bible and the Jerusalem Bible.)
>
> *1 Timothy 1:12–17*

I remember a discussion group many years ago. I was new to the ministry then and very naive. A young college professor made a blasphemous comment I still remember with horror. "Why should I feel indebted to Jesus?" he asked. "I didn't ask him to die for me; besides, I can't think of one thing I need from him." That comment, so shocking thirty-five years ago, now seems almost tame compared to blasphemes I've heard since then. A bit wiser now, I've learned that while few would put their feelings so crudely, many feel as that professor did. The idea that we need a Savior "sounds quaint"; it is hardly a matter to take seriously.

This denial of any need for a Savior is evident in an odd, new practice of self-forgiveness. We're told that guilt and remorse are unhealthy, so we must take a positive attitude and forgive ourselves. An article in a recent issue of *Commonweal* entitled "The Epidemic of Forgiveness" set my wheels to turning.[1] I borrow generously from that article for this sermon. The writer cites the case of Earl Justus, executed in our Commonwealth for the rape and murder of a young woman who was nine months pregnant. That grisly crime was committed just a few miles from here. Before his execution Mr. Justus said in an interview that he was at peace, having forgiven himself for what he'd done. A few years ago Michael Jackson was charged with certain sexual indiscretions. After weeks of depression and the avoidance of public appearances, he announced to his relieved fans that he had forgiven himself and was now ready to get on with his life.

Obviously if we can forgive ourselves we don't need a Savior. And if this is the case, then God is not only incompetent; he is a sadist for leaving his Son to writhe in agony on a cross for spiritual problems we can allegedly handle quite well ourselves.

Our parents and ancestors took no such complacent attitude toward their sin, nor did they doubt their desperate need of God's forgiveness. They hated and feared sin and trembled before the threatening abyss of hell. Yet, knowing the burden of guilt and sin, they also knew the love of a Saviour at depths of the soul which remain unfathomed by us who mistake our barren banalities for real life. And knowing the love of a Savior, they also knew a power of forgiveness that set them free and filled them with a joy unknown to their modern, sophisticated children.

So whence comes this odd idea that we can forgive ourselves? Several thoughts come quickly to mind.

First and foremost is the fact that we don't warm to the idea that we're sinners. Former President Reagan is alleged to have said that he never believed in original sin because it was so uncheery.[2] How degrading to such superior creatures as we fancy ourselves to be to be told that we are sick unto death! So we try to make our sinfulness less heinous with euphemisms that define sin as psychological disorders. "Rape" is now called "aggressive phallic syndrome." "Theft" is "unwarranted transfer of property." No longer can we speak of illegitimacy because the word suggests that fornication and adultery are wrong, while liberated people know it's simply "recreational sex." The unspeakable crime of murdering one's children, which was loathsome to the ancient Greeks, is now explained as a psychological disorder stemming from the murderer having suffered abuse as a child.

Has this new vocabulary improved anything? These euphemistic terms for sin have not made us one bit more healthy or secure or loving. They have instead cut the nerve of moral and spiritual awareness and made it easier to think sin is so insignificant we can forgive ourselves. Thus life grows worse and more dangerous.

American religion is certainly not guiltless in this loss. Ministers have either ceased railing against sin altogether or they've reduced sin to trivialities. Some years ago I was paying for the gasoline I'd just pumped into my near-empty gas tank and overheard a gentleman discoursing on sin. "You know what the worst sins are?" He was talking to the proprietor, and since taking up arms against sin is my business, I wanted to learn where I must go looking for the enemy. "The worst of all sins is using lipstick, smoking cigarettes, drinking coffee, and going to movies." The proprietor's wife, knowing better than he God's love of beauty, said that red paint can make any old barn look better. Since this "moral gadfly" did none of these godless, abominable things, he obviously considered himself a perfect saint.

I wanted to laugh, but I was afraid he was serious, so I quickly and quietly exited the filling station. I learned long ago never to criticize a man's dog or his religion. No doubt he'd gained this profound theological insight from some brainless minister, and no doubt there are churches that teach such idiocy. And it occurred to me that if this is all there is to sin, then Jesus' death was "much ado about nothing" and we might as well forgive ourselves and not bother God with such trivialities.

Another example of religion's propensity for moral suicide! Back in February *Newsweek* devoted one issue to the lamentable loss of a sense of shame in our society and asked, "How do we bring back a sense of right and wrong?" A conservative theologian, John Richard Neuhaus, was quoted. He said that the roots of our modern moral collapse go back, not to the wild indulgences and moral relativisms of the sixties, but to the *Pollyanna-ish* fifties when religion was popular and spiritual leaders like Norman Vincent Peale taught us not to think about bad things in life that depress us, but to think positively.[3] Well, if that's the solution to our human predicament, then clearly we don't need "Jesus the Savior" but "Jesus the divine Cheerleader" or "Jesus the Cosmic Enabler." So why not dismiss the bad things we've done and use Jesus to get on to bigger and better things?

Not to be overlooked in all of this is the eclipse of God in our secular consciousness. So great is our faith in our technical know-how that the movers and shakers in our society consider God to be irrelevant for anything that really matters. John Leo, the religious editor for *U.S. News & World Report* says that when he worked at *Time*, very few reporters learned real life by coming up through the ranks. They came straight out of elitist colleges and universities where they were taught that God is important only to the ignorant masses, not to intelligent people.[4] And Gordon Morino of the University of Virginia says "that the idea of self-forgiveness is a symptom of the secularization process. People for whom the idea of a personal God has become an offense . . . have taken the power of forgiveness upon them-selves."[5] Well, if God is irrelevant, then why not be our own Savior?

The notion of self-forgiveness feeds off a lost sense of the malignant nature of sin. For when moral and spiritual evil are trivialized, as they are in self-forgiveness, moral and spiritual goodness are also trivialized.

Picture a man nurtured in the Presbyterian Faith of his forebears. He drinks in with his mother's milk the conviction that God puts us here on earth to serve him so that, when we depart, the world will be a little bit better. His parents surround him with love and with visions of human great-ness; they scrimp and save so he can have an education that exposes him to the best of western civilization. He is graduated with honors. And what does he do? He throws it all away in a life of indulgence; his only concern, "having fun." Maybe his parents die broken hearted over such tragic waste, and maybe, as a flaccid sot, old before his time, he has a twinge of remorse. He is depressed for a week or two, but one day he snaps out of it and tells his sottish cronies he's forgiven himself.

What would you think? Would such a person be capable of nobility, of courage, of such goodness that others might want to be like him? Hardly. Those who are blind to the dreadful reality of their own sinfulness are also blind to moral and spiritual greatness.

Another example. A vile creature, lower than the beasts, kidnaps and repeatedly rapes a beautiful little twelve-year-old girl who has known nothing but gentleness and love all her life. He is caught, of course, and imprisoned for life. But because of his violence she can never have a baby of her own to hold in her arms, and her delicate spirit is so crushed she remains an emo-tional cripple. If you were that little girl's parents, you would feel nothing but rage every time you thought of that man, and "try as you might, you couldn't forgive him. And then one day you hear that this man has learned to do what you could not do; namely, forgive himself. What would you feel?"[6]

There are two things that make forgiveness real. The first is the purpose of forgiveness. It is not for our mental health but for the restoration of a broken relationship. The second: Only the offended can forgive. Only after we are forgiven by the one we have wronged can we know peace, and even then it cannot be easy. More than that, if we have any spiritual decency, the peace we find can never be the fruit of self-forgiveness, for we are creatures who live by relationships.

In the example just cited, isn't it the little girl's forgiveness that man must have for what he did to her? And isn't it the parents' forgiveness he must have for what he did to their love, their hopes, their dreams? And deeper than this, isn't it God's forgiveness he must have, for isn't God ultimately the one sinned against?

If "the earth is the Lord's and the fullness thereof," then any crime against creation is a crime against the one who created all things in love for his own purposes. Indeed, if each person bears the imprint of God's image, and if the Father of us all counts the very hair of our heads,[7] then any crime done to one of us is a crime against his great fatherly heart. There is no forgiveness unless he first forgives.

Let me tell of another discussion group and another professor. The setting was the Westminster Fellowship Building at Winthrop College in Rock Hill, South Carolina. We were talking about the need to confess our sin. That's the way we wash the grime off our spiritual wounds so the gift of a Savior's forgiveness can reach the hurt and begin its healing, reconciling work. That's the way we strip away our illusions of innocence and victimization so the light of God's truth can banish our darkness. Well, I claimed that Christianity alone takes seriously the confession of sin. A psychology professor quickly said, "That's not true; even Communists confess their sins." He was a committed Methodist, an officer in his church, so he should have known better. I countered that what they confess does not even remotely resemble Christian confession of sin. They merely acknowledge the errors of past governments or the errors of their institutions. The world is full of people ready to confess the mistakes of others, even to confess their own mistakes which they can certainly correct with better information or a new opportunity. But to confess that I have sinned against God and wronged him, to confess that I can do nothing to right that wrong, to confess that beyond the wrong I do to my neighbor or to my own ideals is the wrong I do to the God who loves me, this, I said, only Christianity teaches. And we can know no peace, no wholeness until we are set free by his forgiveness.

Do we need a Savior? Do you need a Savior? "The saying is sure and worthy of full acceptance, that Christ Jesus came into the world to save sinners." But we are blind to the depth of our sin and our need for a Savior until the pure love of God surrounds our hearts and sets us free to know the truth about ourselves.

Is it not true that we never knew how desperately we needed love until we were loved? Is it not also true that we never knew what it means to sin against love until we were loved and forgiven? What is it that keeps us from accepting God's love and forgiveness so our eyes can be opened to the truth about ourselves and we can be free from our great pretensions? Is it that we fear this love will open our eyes to the dreadful depths of our sin? This is surely part of the truth we fear. Or is it that we fear this love may open our eyes to the greatness which can be ours, but which our sin keeps us from reaching? This is also part of the truth we fear. However you answer, the fact remains that Christ Jesus our Lord and Savior rides into Jerusalem to bear our sin on the cross and to free us from its curse. Isn't it time we begin living like those who are forgiven?

10

Hearing the Gospel
for the First Time

Romans 5:6–11; 8:1, 35–39

I WOULD LIKE TO BEGIN WITH A WORD OR TWO ABOUT Paul's letter to the church at Rome. I dare say Romans is not one of your favorite books. The theological argument Paul skillfully develops does not make for devotional snippets or for relaxing bedtime reading; other books of the Bible are much more to our liking. And yet, no other book in this Bible has had a greater influence on the church.

For these two thousand years now, whenever there has been a dramatic rebirth of faith, shaking the church out of her complacency as she needs to be shaken today, Paul's letter to the church at Rome has been the womb of that rebirth. Here, as nowhere else, the gospel of God's grace and the profound implications of that grace are set forth.

I have chosen to read selected verses from Romans. Perhaps some of us may hear its word of truth for the first time and find in it a new life of faith.

The one thing Paul wants us to understand is that our salvation, our spiritual healing, our personal future, and our present and never-ending relation with God, has been settled once and for all in Jesus Christ. It is all a sheer, undeserved gift we can either receive with joy or reject with unbelief. Listen then with believing hearts, for these words are good news to all who know that something is dreadfully amiss at the very heart of life!

For at the very time when we were still powerless, then Christ died for the wicked. Even for a just man one of us would hardly die, though perhaps for a good man one might actually brave death; but Christ died for us while we were yet sinners, and that is God's own proof of his love towards us. And so, since we have now been justified by Christ's sacrificial death, we shall all the more certainly be saved through him from final retribution. For if, when we were God's enemies, we were reconciled to him through the death of his Son, how much more, now that we are reconciled, shall we be saved by his life! But that is not all: we also exult in God through our Lord Jesus, through whom we have now been granted reconciliation.

Romans 5:6–11

The conclusion of the matter is this: there is no condemnation for those who are united with Christ Jesus . . .

Romans 8:1

Then what can separate us from the love of Christ? Can affliction or hardship? Can persecution, hunger, nakedness, peril, or the sword? . . . In spite of all, the overwhelming victory is ours through him who loved us. For I am convinced that there is nothing in death or life, in the realm of spirits or superhuman powers, in the world as it is or the world as it shall be, in forces of the universe, in heights or depths—nothing in all creation that can separate us from the love of God in Christ Jesus our Lord.

Romans 8:35–39 (NEW ENGLISH BIBLE)

Can you trust this word of truth? Then take it into your heart and never again be afraid for your salvation!

May we talk candidly? In all honesty, what do you expect from a sermon? You hope, of course, the sermon will be somewhat interesting, will speak to some need you have, and will be relatively easy to follow. You also hope that a little humor scattered here and there will provide dessert for your ears. I regret to say that I don't always serve it up. There's nothing wrong with such expectations, of course, but what about the sermon's content and purpose?

Maybe you expect the sermon to condemn sin, especially the sins corrupting our society: sex, drugs, robbery, dishonesty, violence, you name it. Or maybe it's the condemnation of social, economic, and racial injustice that you hope to hear. Some people feel they've not heard a real sermon unless the preacher rips into immorality and injustice—the immorality and injustice of others, of course. Sometimes I give you what you want, denouncing the sins of the world because they need to be exposed and condemned. And when we hear such sermons and give our wholehearted assent to the preacher's fulminations, we can go home feeling a little smug because we're not like those rascals the preacher excoriated. But it's not the gospel we hear in such sermons, regardless of how accurate their diagnosis of the sins of others.

Hearing the Gospel for the First Time

There are some Christians who go a step further. It's not the sins of others nor the sins of society they want to have exposed, but their own. They don't think they've heard a real sermon unless they get a moral whipping and go away feeling bad about their continued betrayals of Christ. For them the sermon is like lancing a boil so the poison can be drained. And I sometimes oblige. Too many of my sermons, I fear, are intended to make us feel guilty in hopes we'll all try harder to be good. But it is not the gospel we hear in such sermons, no matter how deserving we are of moral condemnation.

Still others hope for a call to greatness, a sermon that bids us defend the faith at whatever cost while lesser souls shrink from danger; or a sermon that will summon us, a noble, blessed few, to go forth to do battle against evil in us and in the world, while lesser souls hope to be carried to heaven on flowery beds of ease. I've been known to preach such sermons, and I hope they've given courage to fight and not to give up.

Others sermons are expected to provide, not a challenge to greatness, but consolation and the assurance "that God's in his heaven and all's right with the world." You've heard such sermons from this pulpit.

Still other sermons ask only that we ponder some great and noble thought, that we remember the eternal verities that ennoble the human spirit. From time to time I come to this pulpit with only this in mind, and it is good when we sit together around a magnificent truth.

But such sermons, even if they're good, do not set forth the gospel, the good news of God's love. The gospel is not condemnation of sin, neither our own nor that of others; it is not a demand that we try harder to be good; it is not a challenge that we rise up like soldiers of the cross; it is not a kindling of inspiring feelings nor an invitation to think noble thoughts, as good and as necessary as these things are. No, the gospel is the triumphant announcement that in Jesus Christ God has done everything for our salvation, for our spiritual wholeness, for our present and future relationships with him. The gospel is not a demand that we do something or be something or believe something, but the offer of God's incomparable gift of love.

Didn't you notice the verbs in the scripture lesson? The tense of each denotes something finished and done. "We have now been justified by Christ's sacrificial death . . . " "We have now been granted reconciliation." "There is now no condemnation for those who are united with Christ Jesus." "Nothing can separate us from the love of God in Christ Jesus our Lord."

Everything is provided for us by Jesus Christ. We are held in God's grace from beginning to end. How is it then that we can grow up in the church, hear more sermons than we care to remember, and still think that our

61

salvation depends upon what we do or don't do; indeed, worry ourselves sick thinking we have no hope unless we try harder to improve ourselves? This is not Christianity. Has the church failed to proclaim the gospel? Perhaps! Instead of proclaiming again and again the finished work of Christ, we've been told instead what we must do to save our own souls as well as the world, as if we could.

It is time for the gospel to be heard again, maybe for the first time.

Let me tell of three things in which you can trust the grace of God to the uttermost.

First, you can trust that the grace of God has removed the barrier our sin erects to shut him out. Yes, not even our sin can separate us from God's love because in Jesus Christ God proves that his love is stronger than our worst sin. But how slowly this sinks into our unbelieving hearts. I blush to think how I, a preacher of sorts who ought to know such foundational things, am slow to believe that for me, as for you, there is now no condemnation. There are dark seasons of the soul when I fear, just as you fear, that God is not capable of managing my sin: I'm not good enough! I don't really try to be better than I am, nor do I really want to be! I don't pray enough or read the Bible enough or do enough to see God's will done on earth! I've not redressed wrongs I did long ago! I love myself far more than I love God or others! In fact, there are times when I want nothing to do with God. And when I thus condemn myself and let my accusations rule my soul, it's as if I've never heard of Jesus Christ.

So again and again I must hear the gospel anew with the heart of a child, just as you must. At the heart of Christianity is this irrevocable truth: "Sin has been taken away by the sacrifice of Jesus Christ. We have not become good, but before God all the sin of the world has been carried by Jesus Christ, and consequently, although we are still wicked, we are no longer sinners eschatologically before God. Reconciliation has been effected."[1] Our sinfulness cannot now separate us from God. So, for the sake of Christ, do not be burdened with an evil conscience, and do not let the accusations of your conscience or the accusations of the righteous usurp the throne of Christ in your life!

Second, you can trust the grace of God to clothe you in faith when your faith is rags—yes, even when your faith deserts you altogether. For example, we are invited to come to the table of our Lord Jesus Christ in faith, but in whose faith do we come? It is not our faith that makes us worthy to eat this bread and drink this cup. Our faith is weak, faltering, imperfect, unbelieving. "Faith, as John Calvin taught us, is an empty vessel, so that when you approach the table of the Lord, it is not upon your faith that you rely, but upon Christ and his Cross alone."[2] This is the new covenant in his body and blood. His faithfulness clothes our naked souls. "Nothing in my hands I bring, simply to thy cross I cling." So when your faith is weak and doubts devour whatever hope you may have, remember that it is the faithfulness of Jesus Christ that wraps us round and makes us presentable in the presence of God.

And thirdly, we are called to grow in grace, to take up our cross and follow our Lord in loving obedience. So when our obedience fails, we can trust our failed lives to Jesus Christ, who takes upon himself the responsibility of bringing us safely home. "Since we have been justified by Christ's sacrificial death," says Paul, "how much more certain is our salvation since he has been raised from the dead and now lives for us! For if, when we were God's enemies, we were reconciled by his death, shall we not be saved by his life?"

For an earlier generation of Scotland's Presbyterians, there was an oft-read book entitled *Beside the Bonnie Brier Bush*.[3] In one scene a Scottish mother is on her death bed. "Here's me watch and chain," she says to her laddie, who is sobbing at her bedside. "When ye feel the chain bout yir neck it will mind ye o'yir mother's arms." Then as she lays her hand on his head, she goes on: "Ye'll follow Christ, and gin he offers ye his cross, ye'll no refuse it, for he aye carries the heavy end Himself."

His table is spread for you. So come with confidence in his faithfulness, for there is now no condemnation for those who are united with Christ Jesus. Indeed, there is nothing that can separate us from the love of God which is in Christ Jesus our Lord.

11

God's Agenda and Ours

Isaiah 55:8–11; 2 Corinthians 1:20–25

WHAT I WANT TO SAY IS THAT GOD HAS AN AGENDA all his own, and it is usually different from ours. How often we are caught up by great new ideas or programs sure to be the wave of the future, only to discover years later that one of two things has happened! Either the main stream of history left them behind in some remote eddy, or they were radically changed into something far different from their original intent. This is true of history; it is also true of our individual lives. Often it is said, generally with regret, but sometimes with joy: "My life is far different from what I intended!" God's agenda is often quite different from ours.

This seems an appropriate topic for Reformation Sunday. Most thinking people in the sixteenth century would not have given the Protestant Reformation a ghost of a chance against the wealth and power of the Church of Rome. But God must have had plans which eluded the pundits who thought they had their fingers on the pulse of history. So I have chosen two texts for the morning, one from Isaiah and the other from the writings of Paul.

> For my thoughts are not your thoughts, neither are your ways my ways, says the Lord. For as the heavens are higher than the earth, so are my ways higher than your ways and my thoughts than your thoughts. For as the rain and the snow come down from heaven, and return not thither but water the earth, making it bring forth and sprout, giving seed to the sower and bread to the eater, so shall my word be that goes forth from my mouth; it shall not return to me empty, but it shall accomplish that which I purpose, and prosper in the thing for which I sent it.
>
> *Isaiah 55:8–11*

Our second text comes from Paul's writings to the church in Corinth. In the first century who could have dreamed that a crucified Jew from the tiny town of Nazareth would become the hope of the world, or that the cross on which he suffered would become the universal symbol of God's unrelenting love? The wise and the powerful of this world, if they had even heard of this Jesus, would have bet their reputations that he'd be forgotten in a matter of months.

> "Where is the wise man?" asks Paul. "Where is the scribe? Where is the debater of this age? Has not God made foolish the wisdom of the world? For since, in the wisdom of God, the world did not know God through wisdom, it pleased God through the folly of what we preach to save those who believe. For Jews demand signs and the Greeks seek wisdom, but we preach Christ crucified, a stumbling block to Jews and folly to Gentiles, but to those who are called, both Jews and Greeks, Christ the power of God and the wisdom of God. For the foolishness of God is wiser than men, and the weakness of God is stronger than men.
>
> *1 Corinthians 1:20–25*

Recently I've been thinking about some of the items on the agenda of the modern church, and I got to wondering how many would likely make any lasting difference, much less survive more than one generation. And that took me back to my seminary days. It was the beginning of the fifties. We were still haunted by the carnage and devastation of World War II, and we were convinced God had given the church a rare opportunity. New ideas and new challenges were aborning. Few generations of young ministers ever seized the church's leadership with greater hope and confidence.

I'd like to mention some of those things we thought bore great promise.

At the top of our list was the ecumenical movement. A new spirit of cooperation had drawn Christians together during the dark years of war. We had even forged new bonds with Christians struggling to bear a faithful witness in Nazi Germany. If that unity could be preserved it would give tangible hope for peace to a war-weary world. I have vivid memories of the excitement with which ordinary lay people spoke of this as indisputable proof that the Holy Spirit was awakening the church to a new reformation. Now at last Jesus' prayer for the oneness of his disciples, promised to heal the divisions that had rent his church for millenia. What a dream!

Today, forty-five years later, talk of Christian unity will generate little more than a yawn. Churches care more about competition for members than about Jesus' prayer for his church's unity.

Next on our agenda was hope for a new biblical literacy. The Revised Standard Version of the New Testament was published in 1946; the Old Testament in 1952. This was the first significant translation of the Bible into English since the publication of the King James Version in 1611. With a new translation of the holy scriptures into modern English, we were convinced the reading of the Bible and the understanding of the Bible would surpass all previous generations. We dreamed how the world might be changed with dedicated, knowledgeable Christians nurtured on the Word of God. What a dream!

Today, forty-five years later, with new translations of the Bible coming off the press almost yearly, neglect of the Bible and ignorance of the Bible is greater than it's been for centuries. Something besides fresh, new language is needed to turn us to God's Word.

Turning back to the early fifties, there was coupled with our excitement over a new translation of the Bible, a new theology. It was called "biblical theology." Instead of approaching the Bible with Roman Catholic or Lutheran or Calvinist assumptions, instead of reading the Bible through Baptist or Methodist or Episcopal bifocals, it was argued that with the tools of modern scholarship in our hands, an unbiased study of the scriptures would yield the Bible's own theology, the theology holding the Bible together. Here was a serious, intelligent return to the Bible. Suddenly the study of theology was exciting not only for ministers but for lay people as well. What a challenge!

Today, forty-five years later, that quest for a unified theology of the Bible has been discredited, and if you look, you may find the term "biblical theology" as a footnote in some textbook on twentieth-century theological thought. Theologies of narrow interest seem to be the order of the day.

Let me mention a fourth challenge high on our agenda: bringing an end to racial segregation in American society and in the church. This was a clear injustice that cried out for redress. Now that the war was over there was also a renewed zeal for world missions. The world seemed ripe for the gospel. But how, we asked, could we expect the gospel to be credible to people of Asia and Africa if in America the church of Jesus Christ was racially segregated? Almost all the ministers of that generation, at least the ones of my acquaintance, bear emotional scars from that struggle. But it was a worthy crusade.

Looking back now, forty-five years later, I sometimes wonder what direction we hoped an end to segregation would take. Certainly it was an evil that had to end, but the state of race relations today is far removed from anything we had envisioned. We had hoped for better things.

It is indisputable, I think, that new historic movements, even when born of good and pure motives, do quickly go astray. It is as if a malevolent force turns these noble efforts against us.

The ecumenical movement, the possibility of biblical literacy, the quest for a biblical theology, an end to racial segregation—these were all good and noble dreams to challenge the best within us. And few generations of young ministers and young church leaders ever marched through a door of opportunity with such excitement and confidence.

And today? You scan the horizon and you conclude there's nothing comparable stirring in the modern church, nothing that can capture our souls like the dreams of hope and innocence in those "Galahad" days. Today there is excitement in some circles over "inclusive language," as if this will make the gospel more acceptable; excitement over innovative worship to make it more lively: colorful pulpit robes, changes in the order of worship, clever attempts to involve congregational members; excitement over copying the business world: ministers as efficient chief executive officers instead of shepherds, and churches like successful businesses instead of families of faith; excitement over mega-congregations with their "Christian life centers," their smorgasbord of programs to meet every need until such churches look more like religious country clubs than the servants of Christ.

Dreams? There's little in this to grip the soul. It is of such little consequence as not even to awaken Satan from his fitful sleep. And I think it's a safe bet that forty-five years from now Christians will wonder whatever became of these little ripples that were supposed to be the wave of the future.

God's agenda is different from ours. Thank goodness.

But amid all the changes that come and go, amid all the innovative theologies that occupy the stage for a moment in time and then disappear, God's agenda, the gospel, the good news of his love in Christ, remains forever the same and forever tugs at our poor hearts.

Like this telling of it by that teacher of preachers, Paul Scherer. Listen!

"The cross is the whispered word of a God travel-stained and footsore, seeking someone, ever away from home, whispering a name." Is it your name? "They say the search began in a garden in the cool of the day among the trees where a man stood, trembling and ashamed, and a woman with him, listening to a voice that seemed at first like the sad murmur of leaves. 'Adam, Adam! Where art thou my son?' It may be that you spell the name of the garden 'E-d-e-n'; but the God who walked there"[1] now whispers your name and mine in a Garden where an empty tomb opens wide the door to our Father's house.

Another comment on the timelessness of God's agenda! During my recent study leave I finally got into a book that has long been on my shelf. The author, a lifelong friend of C. S. Lewis, comments on the effort of some to find new and trendy ways to make Jesus palatable to fickle generations. Somehow Clive Staple Lewis was above all this. Somehow he knew that the story of Jesus itself is of such mystery and wonder as to put us all on our knees in adoring silence. Listen!

> "Neither your sages nor your dunderheads, your kings nor your peasants, your shopkeepers nor your ordinary clerks and householders (that is to say, none of us) can cling to, let alone adore, The Man for Others," as some now call Jesus, "or The Ground of Being," as some now call God, "or Caring and Sharing," a motherly euphemism for the hidden God who comes to us in Jesus Christ. "No. We mortals must come to that odd place where the poor Jewish girl heard the archangelic salutation, and to the Creche, and to the Cross and to the grave that has a corpse missing from it." Somehow in these particular spots, humble and unlettered men, women and children find "themselves kneeling next to St. Augustine, St. Thomas Aquinas, St. Thomas More, Pascal,"[2] Martin Luther, John Calvin, C. S. Lewis and a host of saints in white robes no man can number.

Thanks be to God, "the foolishness of God is wiser than men, and the weakness of God is stronger than men." So tell me, when the waves we hope to ride into the future run out to nothing in forgotten eddies, are you foolish enough and weak enough to hear the pounding of the surf on that blessed shore where we will all be home again—forever? If so, then will prosper, as surely as the night gives way to dawn, the new life for which God sends his unfailing Word into your heart. Trust him!

12

A Maundy Thursday Homily

John 13

JESUS, KNOWING THAT THE FATHER HAD GIVEN ALL things into his hands, and that he had come from God and was going to God, rose from supper, laid aside his garments, and girded himself with a towel. Then he poured water into a basin, and began to wash the disciples' feet, and to wipe them with the towel with which he was girded. . . . When he had washed their feet, and taken his garments, and resumed his place, he said to them, . . . "If I then, your Lord and Teacher, have washed your feet, you also ought to wash one another's feet. . . . Truly, truly, I say to you, a servant is not greater than his master; nor is he who is sent greater than he who sent him. If you know these things, blessed are you if you do them."

Selected Verses from John 13

Whenever I read this scripture I think of a story told by my son Bill. It was Easter last year, and a lady, a member of his church, told about going to a Maundy Thursday service in a little sectarian church that practiced foot-washing. Said the lady, "Have you ever thought what you'd do if you're wearing pantyhose?" That has nothing to do with the sermon, but I offer it as warning if you are ever invited to a foot-washing ceremony.

A few years ago Martin Marty, the man who probably knows more than anyone else about American church history, was asked to write something to be deposited in a time capsule. The City of Chicago invited some national leaders to put down what they believed would be the dominant movement over the next century. When the capsule is opened sometime in the twenty-first century it will be interesting to see who had the best crystal ball. For his part, Martin Marty said the next century will be dominated by tribalism. Tribalism! The dream of peace and world cooperation that followed the agony of World War II will be cast aside as each country, each ethnic group, each religious movement and each special interest angrily demands its own rights, regardless of the injury done to others. At some point in the next century, after decades of strife and the breaking apart of societies, the world will grow weary of conflict and chaos. And then, once again, humankind will understand that we cannot survive as human beings unless we are willing to serve others, even to sacrifice for others. And from that will come once more the dream of a world united in peace.

That is a grim prediction, but what if Marty is right? Think about it! Look at world events and you see tribalism everywhere. And it grows uglier: economic tribalism, ethnic tribalism, cultural tribalism, educational tribalism, religious tribalism. It's us against the world. Add to that our individual selfishness that grows unchecked in our wicked hearts, and the picture of Jesus, kneeling to wash the feet of his disciples, is so foreign to our habits of life as to be almost incomprehensible. Incomprehensible? But what if the only thing that can keep us from devouring one another is his Spirit in us, burning away our pampered selfishness and empowering us to serve others, especially those closest and dearest to us! If we were ready to do that, if only for our closest and dearest, what a different world this would be!

But don't expect the angry spokesmen of tribalism to tip their hats to Jesus the foot-washer, much less to Jesus the crucified. We alone are entrusted with the privilege of knowing the One from whom all caring flows. And maybe, just maybe, we who gather here in his name, together with a million-and-one nameless little congregations of Christians like us all across the world, are indeed God's elect. And what if the greatest gift we can give to the world's future is simply to keep alive this spirit: caring for one another, and serving one another as Jesus Christ serves the best in us! If this is so, then this Supper shared with Christ our Lord and with each other in his Spirit, may do more to ensure the world's future than a hundred momentous decisions made in Washington or Moscow or Tokyo.

Years ago, when I was a college student, I heard Joseph Sizo, a noted minister of a former generation. He preached a sermon on this text entitled "The Towel or The Tin Cup." As you meditate on your relationship with members of this family of faith, ask how often you come with cup in hand, expecting a social or religious handout, and how often you come with towel in hand expecting to serve others as Christ has served us.

Let us pray! "O heavenly Father, give me a heart like the heart of Jesus Christ, a heart more ready to minister than to be ministered unto, a heart moved with compassion toward the weak and the oppressed, a heart set upon the coming of your kingdom in this world. Amen."[1]

13

A Theological Question About Health Care

Genesis 3:1–7; Mark 2:1–12

I HAVE CHOSEN TWO SCRIPTURES. THE FIRST IS FROM THE third chapter of Genesis. It tells how we human creatures are seduced into thinking we can ignore, even defy, the limits of our creaturehood. The second is from the second chapter of the Gospel According to Mark. It tells how Jesus showed that he had authority to forgive sin.

You may wonder what these two scriptures have to do with each other, much less with the current debate about health care. I hope I can satisfy your curiosity by pulling them together and offering a suggestion about their relevance. Let me also say that if you're expecting these scriptures to provide a "God-given" answer to health-care reform, you're going to be totally disappointed. There is no infallible, "God-given" answer. But what they do offer is something far more important. They invite us to consider the meaning of life, the "why?" of our existence that should undergird all debate about health care. They also raise critical questions about what we Americans naively assume to be the meaning of life and the priorities of life. At issue is whether we who profess to be Christians are up to hearing this Word of God. Listen then with curious and believing hearts!

Now the serpent was more subtle than any other wild creature that the Lord God had made. He said to the woman, "Did God say, 'You shall not eat of any tree of the garden'?" And the woman said to the serpent, "We may eat of the fruit of the trees of the garden; but God said, 'You shall not eat of the fruit of the tree which is in the midst of the garden, neither shall you touch it, lest you die.'" But the serpent said to the woman, "You will not die. For God knows that when you eat of it your eyes will be opened, and you will be like God, knowing good and evil."

71

So when the woman saw that the tree was good for food, and that it was a delight to the eyes, and that the tree was to be desired to make one wise, she took of its fruit and ate; and she also gave some to her husband, and he ate. Then the eyes of both were opened, and they knew that they were naked; and they sewed fig leaves together and made themselves aprons.

Genesis 3:1–7

And when he returned to Capernaum after some days, it was reported that he was at home. And many were gathered together, so that there was no longer room for them, not even about the door; and he was preaching the word to them. And they came, bringing to him a paralytic carried by four men. And when they could not get near him because of the crowd, they removed the roof above him; and when they had made an opening, they let down the pallet on which the paralytic lay. And when Jesus saw their faith, he said to the paralytic, "My son, your sins are forgiven." Now some of the scribes were sitting there, questioning in their hearts, "Why does this man speak thus? It is blasphemy! Who can forgive sins but God alone?" And immediately, Jesus, perceiving in his spirit that they thus questioned within themselves, said to them, "Why do you question thus in your hearts? Which is easier, to say to the paralytic, 'Your sins are forgiven,' or to say, 'Rise, take up your pallet and walk'? But that you may know that the Son of man has authority on earth to forgive sins"—he said to the paralytic— "I say to you, rise, take up your pallet and go home." And he rose, and immediately took up the pallet and went out before them all; so that they were all amazed and glorified God, saying, "We never saw anything like this!"

Mark 2:1–12

Like most of you, I'm sure, I find the current health-care debate bewildering. Senator Mitchell's bill, only one of several up for grabs, covers fourteen hundred pages.[1] "The subject is complicated to start with," writes Steven Waldman in *Newsweek*, "but lawmakers have made it more confounding by obscuring reality. So far, advocates for the major bills have two things in common: (1) they all claim they can cure the health-care system without sacrifice and (2) they are all wrong."[2]

Admittedly, something needs to be done. But what? We all complain about skyrocketing health costs, we all believe that everyone should have access to health care, but none of us is willing to make the sacrifices necessary for genuine reform. We want reform, but we want someone else to bear the cost. And what is more, lawmakers who know us only too well go out of their way to obscure the real cost of bills they author.

My sermon this morning is not so much about health-care reform as it is about us, about sinful human nature. We want more and more done for us: by the church, by the school, by business, and especially by government. But not only do we refuse to consider the cost of our wants; we also refuse to consider the theological implications of our wants. I hope the sermon will prod us to do this.

An editorial in *Commonweal* led me to write this sermon. It raises theological questions about health-care reform which are studiously ignored in the current legislative debates and in the media coverage of these debates. Listen to these thoughtful words of truth; they suggest things we prefer not to consider.

> Sickness, the full impact of which is physical, emotional, spiritual and social—is always a larger subject than the medical means we have devised to treat it. The diseases that make us ill, will finally take us from life. Finally each of us will die no matter the state of medical progress—or health-care reform.

> Why illness? Why death? Why this death that takes me or the one I love? It would be foolish to imagine that the larger meaning of illness . . . could make its way into the polling and posturing that go with the legislative debate on national health-care reform. Yet this larger meaning is implicit in questions about the limits to medical intervention and limits to the provision of health-care services. They are implicit because there are diseases, or stages in the course of a disease, for which there is no medical remedy, and others for which the cost of treatment would be simply prohibitive. It is partly because our society is unwilling and unable to set limits—even in instances where treatment is clearly futile—that medical care costs have risen and, in some measure, created the crisis that health-care reform is trying to relieve. Isn't this because we cannot ask why?

> A dramatic example: Cancer patients are successfully suing insurance companies, forcing them to pay for experimental procedures in a last effort to fight terminal conditions. Sympathetic juries have been unwilling to enforce contractual restrictions on such treatments, especially perhaps because the patient is dying. This has resulted in at least

some companies agreeing to pay for treatment simply on the threat of a legal suit. There is no evidence that patients or families are better off. In the meantime, insurance premiums increase for everyone, and the cost of medical care heads steadily upward. Is it realistic to suppose that health-care reform will or can force Americans to face up to the question of limits? If one litigant has forced an insurance firm to surrender, why not all cases similarly situated? If your dying child, why not mine?[3]

I shudder before such a question. Were it my child or my spouse, I know how I would answer. And because no one can or will face such a dreadful question, health costs spiral.

The text from Genesis is about our refusal to accept the limits of our created existence, especially the limit of death. "You will not die," whispered the serpent. "For God knows that when you eat of it your eyes will be opened, and you will be like God, knowing good and evil." The promise of immortality and the defiance of death has always been the serpent's lie. And it is a very short distance as the soul flies from our refusal to face the limit of death to our refusal to accept any other limits. We want to believe there is nothing we cannot do, nothing we cannot achieve with our great wisdom and power. We want to be like God, the limitless One, not the creatures that we are.

Our inability to accept the limit of death has a direct bearing on our health-care crisis. For us, and for the medical profession, death has become the ultimate evil, not rebellion against God which the Bible defines as the ultimate evil, but biological death. Consequently physical death must be fought and postponed by any means and at whatever cost. This being so, should we not see theological implications in the fact that sixty percent of Medicare costs occur in the last year of peoples' lives, even when they are hopelessly ill?

Another limit we refuse to face is the consequences of our personal behavior. Abuse the body God has given you and it follows as the night the day that you will eventually pay for it in poor health. But we think we can dodge this inexorable logic. I have no exact figures, but the cost of treating illnesses resulting from our own irresponsible behavior must be staggering. My guess is that the treatment of illnesses resulting from excessive use of tobacco, the abuse of alcohol and drugs, unhealthy diets, sexual promiscuity, and the refusal to exercise consumes far more medical dollars than the treatment of purely genetically caused illnesses. As I say, I have no proof of this; it is only a guess. But the point I want to make is that we actually think we can ignore this fact, this limit, that certain behaviors result in predictable consequences. On the one hand we assume science will always bail us out so we don't have to be careful or responsible. Why diet? A pill will solve the problem of obesity. Why refrain from sexual fun and games? The great god science will find a cure for any disease we may pick up along the way. And on the other hand, we choose to ruin our bodies, and then expect everyone else to bear the cost of finding a cure or making us well.

One more limit, a very crucial one. In the words of a very learned physician, "There is a finite amount of money available for health care, while the need for health care can be infinite."[4] It is no wonder the lawmakers try to obscure the real cost of health-care reform; it is awesome. Spending for health care already claims twenty-one percent of federal spending. Even if nothing is done to reform the system, and health care continues on its present course, this figure will jump to more than thirty-three percent of federal spending within ten years. And the federal debt keeps growing year after year apart from this. Consider too the inability of government statisticians to predict future costs. In 1965, government statisticians predicted that in 1990 Medicare hospital insurance would cost nine billion dollars. The actual cost in 1990 turned out to be sixty-seven billion dollars. That figure comes not from Ross Perot but from the House Ways and Means Committee.

We brash Americans want to believe there's nothing we can't do if we put our minds to it. But according to the biblical faith, this is what the Greeks called *hubris*, overweening pride, the refusal to bow before God and the limits within which we must learn to live. But what if we must learn to live within limits to survive as a society, as a liveable earth? How would it change our expectations about health care if we had to accept the limits in which God has set our lives? That is neither a medical question nor a political question but a theological question that challenges the reality of our faith.

I must comment on the story of the paralytic. I want to make only one point. The point of the story is not the cure of paralysis, but the authority of Jesus to forgive sin. No one was impressed with the healing. That's incidental to the main thrust of the story. Healings of this sort seem to have been a common occurrence in that day. No, the thing that amazed everyone was Jesus' claim to forgive sin. To the scribes and Pharisees this was unmitigated blasphemy; to the disciples, proof of God's gracious presence in this Jesus. It was simply to prove that he had authority to forgive sins that he told the man to take up his pallet and walk.

Let me clarify a few things before I comment on the primacy of forgiveness and its significance for us. We must not conclude from this, as many are wont to do, that sickness is the result of sin. On other occasions Jesus flatly rejected this bad idea. Nor can we conclude from this story, as many are wont to do, that it was the sick man's faith that made him well. If there's any evidence of faith in this story, it is that of the men who carried him and let him down through the roof. There's no mention of faith on the part of the paralytic. Nor can we conclude from this story, as some are wont to do, that forgiveness is necessary for healing. It is possible to know forgiveness without being healed. This seems to have been the case for the Apostle Paul with his thorn in the flesh. It is also possible for one to be healed and not forgiven.[5] And of such a state we could ask, "What does it profit a man to be in perfect health but to have death festering at the core of his being?"

No, what we must hear in this story is that for Jesus and for the New Testament, man's most serious problem is not sickness but sin. So this story is a disturbing reminder that forgiveness, God's gracious healing of the human spirit, is far more important than physical health. But to us who have made health an ultimate good and who have no sense of sin this is incomprehensible. Does this mean we are wiser than Jesus and the New Testament, or does it mean that with our great scientific know-how we may have forgotten the fundamental truth about life? Forgiveness, a new and right relationship with God, is far more important than healing.

What is the primary issue for your life?

No sermon is complete without a few practical applications. So I want to say that regardless of the final health-care reform bill adopted by government, there are some things we can do as individual Christians. You and I can and must do a better job of living healthy lives: exercise, diet, the avoidance of behaviors and substances that destroy health. Second, we can sign a living will to avoid needless, heroic measures to preserve our own life when death is unavoidable, and we can make sure our loved ones understand and honor our wishes. A third thing! We can and should ponder the vexing question, "How much is enough when it comes to health care?" especially with such technological wonders in the doctor's bag of tricks and with unbelievable wonders yet to come. And more than pondering it, we need to talk about it with loved ones and friends. Such things are concrete expressions of our faith.

And I cannot let this moment pass without asking a question which, perhaps more than any others, challenges the integrity of our faith. What does it mean for us who piously claim to follow him who came not to be served but to serve, especially the helpless and defenseless—what does it mean that we are never bothered by our eagerness to see billions spent for exotic cures for us while billions of our fellow earthlings go without the most basic health care? I'm sure there is neither a rational answer to such a question, nor an economic answer, and certainly not a political answer. But does that exhaust the realities by which we live? What of the truth incarnate in Jesus Christ? Anyone who honestly believes we will all stand before the judgment seat of God to answer for our use of his gifts, cannot simply shrug off this question with the comment: "Well, this is just the way things are!" For by the grace of God his kingdom can and will make all things different from what they are.

I want to close with what may sound like a strange comment. Sometimes I wonder why you come to church. If I, or any minister, is faithful to the Word of God, then we must attack cultural beliefs you accept as "self-evident;" we must expose the dark side of hallowed American virtues; we must unmask the illusions and empty promises offered us daily by those in power; we must constantly remind you that we must learn to live within limits; and we must continually remind you of the grim reality of death, of your own death. Isn't this what we must do if we are faithful? No wonder the world with its bright-shining agenda writes us off as irrelevant!

But what if it is true? What if the only way into the future is to love and serve God before all else and to embrace joyfully and trustingly the limits in which he sets our lives? If it is true, then to ignore the limits he has set is to trifle with our souls. But more important than the preservation of our souls, subduing our proud lives to the limits God has set will remind the world that faith does matter. If not for the world, at least for us, and then perhaps the world may wish to ask what it is that makes us different.

14

Life Work

Ecclesiastes 1:2–3; 2:4–6, 18–21; 11:12b; 3:12–13; 1 Corinthians 15:54–58

L ET US NOW HEAR THE SOBERING WORDS THAT COME TO US from Koheleth, the Preacher. His testimony speaks of toil, wisdom, and foolishness—for him all human labor was an exercise in sheer vanity.

Vanity of vanities, says the Preacher, . . . All is vanity. What does man gain by all the toil at which he toils under the sun?

Ecclesiastes 1:2–3

I made great works; I built houses and planted vineyards for myself; I made myself gardens and parks, and planted in them all kinds of fruit trees.

Ecclesiastes 2:4–6

I hated all my toil in which I had toiled under the sun, seeing that I must leave it to the man who will come after me; and who knows whether he will be a wise man or a fool? Yet he will be master of all for which I toiled and used my wisdom. . . . This also is vanity. So I turned about and gave my heart up to despair over all the toil of my labors, . . . because sometimes a man who has toiled with wisdom and knowledge and skill must leave all to be enjoyed by a man who did not toil for it. This also is vanity and a great evil.

Ecclesiastes 2:18–21

Of making many books there is no end, and much study is a weariness to the flesh.

Ecclesiastes 11:12b

I know that there is nothing better for (the children of men) than to be
happy and enjoy themselves as long as they live; also it is God's gift to
man that everyone should eat and drink and take pleasure in his toil.

Ecclesiastes 3:12–13

Listen now to the bright shining difference Christ's resurrection can
make of the work God gives us to do!

When the perishable puts on the imperishable, and the mortal puts on
immortality, then shall come to pass the saying that is written: "Death
is swallowed up in victory." "O death, where is thy victory? O death,
where is thy sting?" The sting of death is sin, and the power of sin is the
law. But thanks be to God, who gives us the victory through our Lord
Jesus Christ. Therefore, my beloved brethren, be steadfast, immovable,
always abounding in the work of the Lord, knowing that in the Lord
your labor is not in vain.

1 Corinthians 15:54–58

Life Work is the title of a new book by Donald Hall, poet and writer, who
resides in New Hampshire.[1] Unlike Koheleth, for whom work was "vanity of
vanities," and unlike many today who hate their work, Donald Hall loves his
work. Just when his children were preparing to enter college, he resigned as
a tenured professor at a great midwestern university to be free to pursue his
calling as a writer. Mornings he can hardly wait to get to his desk to fashion
words into new forms of meaning and reality, just as a sculptor takes clay or
marble and fashions beauty. Donald Hall is known to rework his poetry three
or four hundred times before he feels it's fit for publication. For him it is a
work of love. Such perfection is beyond the comprehension of this poor minister for whom it's "ready or not" each Sunday.

Donald Hall once asked the British sculptor Henry Moore the secret of
life. Moore was in his eighties and still in love with his work of fashioning
beauty out of inert material. "The secret of life," he said, "is to have a task,
something you devote your entire life to, something you bring everything to,
every minute of the day for your whole life. And the most important thing
is—it must be something you cannot possibly do."[2] Don't we achieve our
best when we reach for the stars?

I understand a tiny bit of this love for one's work. Often I say to myself,
"Bill Klein, you are one of the luckiest men alive; you get paid for doing what

you love to do." It's true, of course, that desolate periods set in when the springs of creativity are a dry hole. And there are aspects of ministry I would gladly give up, like onerous managerial duties—I was not cut out to be anyone's boss or supervisor—and fruitless meetings. I accept that as part of the territory, however. So taking it all together, I wouldn't swap my work for any other on earth, and my love affair with my life work mellows with age. Loving it as I do, I sometimes fear that when approaching the "pearly gates" God may say of me, as Jesus said of the Pharisees, "Truly, I say . . . they (already) have their reward."[3]

My joy in my life work is set against the joylessness that so many experience. I think of the millions who hate their work, and of millions more sunk in despair because they have no work. I think of people who once loved their work but love it no more, of people late to arrive at work and early to leave because they do not love it, of people who do only what their job description requires, and that from an onerous sense of duty. No job is immune to the loss of joy and meaning, however, not even mine. And I am quite sure I'd come to hate my work if it meant standing at an auto assembly line or peering through a microscope day after day, or having to be a minister if the ministry were not my calling, or if I had to live in fear that my company to which I'd given my best might be the victim of a hostile takeover and I'd be out of work. So I really do know how fortunate I am.

But I will not speak to those who hate their work, or to those who despair because they have no work, though both are tragedies of major proportions. No, I'm concerned about us lucky ones who love our work or at least claim to love it. And what I want to ask is this: Did Koheleth know something about life work we are yet to discover, that in the end it is only "vanity of vanities?"

Let me make one side comment before I go on. While Koheleth could say that in the end work is "vanity of vanities," he never advised laziness. For the lazy he had only contempt. And while I'm on the subject, let me make an additional aside about the Protestant work-ethic that was often maligned during the flamboyant sixties when indulgence was king. We would do well to remember that time and again this Protestant work-ethic has lifted millions of Protestants out of poverty's grip. Nowhere does the Bible condone laziness or indulgence.

Now that I've gotten that off my chest, back to the theme of this sermon: the seductive promise of the lifework we love! Sometimes when the springs of my creativity are a dry hole, I look at this love of my life and I catch a glimpse of her dark, cynical face. What if she turns against me and betrays me like a faithless, adulterous wife? Is this the discovery Koheleth made, that even successful work is "vanity of vanities" because it can never give us what we want and need?

Does our work always betray us? If so, this is not what God intends. God intends for us to derive satisfaction from the work he gives us to do. Koheleth knows this in spite of his cynicism. " . . . it is God's gift to man that everyone . . . should take pleasure in all his toil." So in the creation story God entrusts the garden to Adam and gives him the task of tending it as his vice regent, as his personal representative with all the dignity and freedom that go with it. Can we poor mortals have any greater dignity? Only later, in this ancient story, does work become a curse. The tending of God's garden became oppressive toil when Adam decided—and Adam is every one of us—that he'd be the master of his own life and the master of the garden as well, instead of God's loving servant. And when it is no longer God's garden, and we are no longer his servants, then everything about our work is drained of joy and meaning.

No longer do the fruits of our labor give happiness. After all, the fruit of Koheleth's toil was enviable: houses and gardens and slaves and herds and gold. Do not all the things our work enables us to possess and do give sufficient reason to love our work? In our commercial society we work to buy and work more to buy more. Can one love his work in a commercial society? Do not the values of a commercial society assume that work is a burden—at best, bearable only for its material fruit?

But then one day Koheleth scanned all that he possessed and his soul was still empty. Did he suddenly realize that his possessions, the fruit of his toil, now owned him? Added to this was the realization that the years were catching up with him and that his vast estate would fall into the hands of another. Would it all fall into the hands of a fool, a wastrel? Or worse, might it be devoured by wasteful, tax-hungry politicians? But whether into the hands of fools or the children of wisdom, everything for which he'd toiled would be his no longer. And suddenly he hated the toil he'd hoped would give him happiness.

And we? We are not immune to his discovery that one can own the whole world and yet have a starved soul; that one can be envied by one's neighbors and yet weep inwardly. We know that, but we still want more, refusing to believe that nothing can give us joy and satisfaction once we arrogantly claim that the garden is ours to do with as we please, and that we are masters of our own fate.

Maybe possessions interest us not at all. Maybe we have foregone wealth and possessions simply for the fame that will be ours—a scientific discovery that comes after years of research, a book that makes the best seller list, a reputation as a great teacher. To do something that brings dignity and honor to your name is for many far greater than wealth. So when Sir Lawrence Olivier died, someone wrote that Arnold Schwarzenegger probably earns more money from one film than Sir Lawrence earned over a lifetime of acting. But, said the writer, money could not buy the honor given to Lawrence Olivier: to be laid to rest in the Poet's Corner of Westminster Abbey.

For whom do we really work? Certainly not for God, in spite of our pious Presbyterian protestations about the glory of God, though perhaps we are never totally unmindful of the honor due him. But were we serious about even a third of the glory going to him, would we cast envious eyes and caustic words at friends and colleagues whose labors are more successful than ours? Would we not rejoice that God is being glorified through them? And have we not made an idol of our work? Notice it is always "my work" or "our work," not God's! And haven't we bet our lives on the belief that work and the success it gives offer the only way we can prove to ourselves and to others that we have dignity and worth? The story of Adam is our story; the dignity God gives is not good enough; we must reach for the stars, and according to our own rules. No wonder our work always betrays us like an adulterous spouse. Is this another reason why Koheleth became cynical about work, because it came to him that love for one's life work is often little more than love of self? *?*

I sometimes try to read the sermons of pulpit masters from the past: Savonarola, John Donne, Martin Luther, Phillips Brooks. Their sermons once kindled flames of hope and love in faithful Christians. Those sermons are now as lifeless as cold ashes, for they belong to another time and place, and the voices that made them live have fallen silent. And I am fool enough to think my pitiful life work will make my name memorable a year after I'm dead and gone? "Time, like an ever-rolling stream, bears all its sons away . . . "[4] as well as their sweet labors.

And then, as if this realization were not enough to rob our life work of delight, the numbing reality of death reduces everything we do, the best of it and no less the worst of it, to nothing.

Donald Hall is afflicted with cancer. Was there a time, not too long ago, when he would read books ravenously and then stack them on his desk? I know the practice. Later you will read them with care and digest their thoughts the better to fashion them into beauty. Does he now hate those stacks of books as they wait for eyes that may never feast upon their blessed words?

Donald Hall says that the last time he was in England he visited Henry Moore the great sculptor, that old friend who had the secret of life. Henry

Moore sat in a chair, tended by nurses, a note pad in hand upon which he scribbled meaningless lines. The ravages of time had robbed him of his creative genius before he could shape his best dreams into form—this man who wanted to be another Michaelangelo. Life work!

Well, you can say that great things are accomplished only when we reach for the stars, only when we love the challenge of striving for something we cannot possibly do. But, in the end, as Koheleth knew, even this is "vanity of vanities." Unless—unless it really is true that our Lord Jesus Christ, full of grace for the likes of us, takes the work we love, separates out of our successes and our failures anything he finds useful, and then says to souls, chastened and purified by death, by his death and by ours: "Well done, good and faithful servant. . . . "

It will not be because of our noble efforts and accomplishments, whether great or small, that he will say this, but simply because his life work is to love us and to fashion us into loving servants of our Father in heaven. Is there anything else that can save our life work? Is there anything else that can give us dignity that not even death can erase?

"Therefore, my beloved, . . . be steadfast, immovable, always abounding in the work of the Lord, knowing that in the Lord your labor is not in vain." Never!

15

Reformed Spirituality

Colossians 1:9–14; 2:6–7

M
AYBE I NEED TO DEFINE THE WORDS IN THE SERMON
title. The word "Reformed" distinguishes our theological tradition
from Roman Catholic and Lutheran and sectarian traditions.
Reformed is almost a synonym for Presbyterian. Both the Reformed churches
of Europe and the Presbyterian churches of the English-speaking world trace
their roots to the Reformation in Switzerland in the sixteenth century. The
word "spirituality" has to do with the daily life of faith, with living by the
Holy Spirit's guidance, with the experience of God's presence.

With this brief introduction, I invite you to hear the lesson. Paul is
writing to the Christians of Colossae, offering pastoral direction for living
Christian lives.

And so, from the day we heard of it, we have not ceased to pray for you,
asking that you may be filled with the knowledge of his will in all spiritual wisdom and understanding, to lead a life worthy of the Lord, fully
pleasing to him, bearing fruit in every good work and increasing in the
knowledge of God. May you be strengthened with all power, according
to his glorious might, for all endurance and patience with joy, giving
thanks to the Father, who has qualified us to share in the inheritance
of the saints in light. He has delivered us from the dominion of darkness and transferred us to the kingdom of his beloved Son, in whom we
have redemption, the forgiveness of sins.

Colossians 1:9–14

As therefore you received Christ Jesus the Lord, so live in him, rooted
and built up in him and established in the faith, just as you were taught,
abounding in thanksgiving.

Colossians 2:6–7

84

Reformed Spirituality

You've noticed it I'm sure, a growing hunger for spiritual reality. This hunger is clearly evident among Christians. Books on prayer, books on "finding God," and books on tapping into the Holy Spirit's power were never more popular. Outside the church this hunger is evident in the many New-Age movements which draw heavily upon an Americanized brand of Buddhism with an emphasis on meditation. These New-Age movements also draw upon a modern, elitist brand of Native American religion: a return to the earth, a quest for the secrets of nature. Have you noticed how popular angels have suddenly become? Some months ago both *Time* and *Newsweek* carried feature articles on angels. Interest in angels always seems to increase when God seems remote or too complicated to bother with.

Howard Rice says that "one of the major causes of the search for religious experience is a sense that modern life has become flat and without passion or a sense of purpose."[1]

Many people have become serious in their search for a living and vital relationship with God because they feel empty. In a confusing world, in which there seems to be very little that one can trust, many people seek the certainty of God's nearness and reliability which only a direct sense of God's presence can bring."[2]

But what kind of experience of God's presence should we seek? Is every alleged experience of God valid? Obviously not. Look at the lives twisted by modern cults claiming to lead the unwary to God. But what of the spirituality of long, established religions? Is the spiritual path of Buddhism more fruitful than the path of Christianity? Or what about the different kinds of spirituality within Christianity itself? As the sermon title suggests, what is considered a normative experience of Christ differs in the various Christian traditions.

I want to suggest four emphases that are special for Reformed/Presbyterian spirituality. There is, first of all, a special understanding of the importance of the Lord's Day, of the covenant community coming together for worship to be nurtured by the Word of God. While the importance of private prayer and private Bible study can never be ignored, this can never be a substitute for corporate worship with the family of faith, the covenant community. This is one reason why Presbyterians do not ordinarily administer baptism privately but as part of the worshiping community.

Also, for us, every Sunday is meant to be a joyful celebration of Christ's resurrection. We worship on Sunday, the first day of the week, instead of on Saturday, the Jewish Sabbath, the seventh day of the week. This should cast

85

our worship in a joyful, festive mood. This rich truth is often obscured by Sabbatarian legalists who burden us with so many "thou shalt nots" that Sunday is stripped of joy. Maybe this is why so many avoid Sunday worship. Our model for Sunday is not the Jewish Sabbath with its many prohibitions, but the excitement of Jesus' resurrection and the promise of creation restored to its joy and beauty. This means, then, that worship should be a time for joyfully remembering all God has done for us and of an eager anticipation of a future in which Christ will be all in all. This being so, shouldn't a church picnic with adults and children playing together be more appropriate for Sunday than sitting alone at home praying bloodless prayers with a long, pinched face? Reformed spirituality can never countenance a private piety that absents us from the joy of a worshiping community.

Why is emphasis on the Lord's Day important? Well, if the rending of the human community into violent, hate-filled factions is a major threat to the world, and if the worshiping community is meant to be God's way of showing the world how human beings can live together joyfully, then private devotions alone are not going to be of much help in healing a shattered world.

There is, secondly, an emphasis upon intellectual life in the service of God. All of the leaders of the Reformation in Switzerland were humanist scholars, children of the Renaissance. For them the rediscovery of the original languages of scripture, together with the wisdom of ancient Greece and Rome, and the writings of the early church fathers were profoundly liberating. So at its best the Reformed faith has always challenged us to think. Consequently, Reformed spirituality has never appealed to the intellectually lazy. Consequently Reformed spirituality has always been suspicious of emotionalism that avoids critical thought.

"Christian faith is no sedative for world-weary souls, no satchelful of ready answers to the deepest questions of life. Christian faith invariably prompts questions, sets an inquiry in motion, fights the inclination to accept things as they are, continually calls in question unexamined assumptions about God, ourselves, and our world."[3] "Human life ceases to be human, not when we do not have all the answers, but when we no longer have the courage to ask the really important questions."[4]

Reformed spirituality, opposed as it is to much that passes for piety in the modern world, calls us to keep growing our minds for the glory of God.

Why is this emphasis on the mind important? Well, if in this day of television and instant communication, it is easy to be misled by demagoguery with its half truths, its lies and its illusions, the world needs Christians who can think and ask critical questions.

There is, thirdly, an emphasis upon moral discipline. An experience of God's presence fills us with a sense of peace and well-being, but it is also a source of profound fear and discomfort. In his presence we are deeply aware of our own sin and the sin of the world, and we know that to be faithful to him we must do something about it. Thus Reformed spirituality has no use for the modern notion that warm fuzzy feelings are proof of God's presence. Being close to God requires that we strive to be more like Christ our Lord, struggling against everything in us that is unworthy of his name.

Some of you are familiar with the name, George F. Keenan, statesman and scholar. He was of Scotch and English parentage. From his birth he was nurtured on the Reformed faith; it shaped his private and public life. I cite George Keenan because of the qualities of life instilled in him by his Presbyterian/Reformed heritage.

> In the outward sense he seeks to live by such things as generosity, kindness, courtesy, understanding, patience, and certain kinds of loyalty. In the inward sense . . . modesty, self-control, self-discipline, sensitivity to the dictates of conscience, awareness of one's own imperfections and the effort to struggle against them, humbleness in the face of one's failures.[5]

Modesty? Self-control? Self-discipline? Sensitivity to the dictates of conscience? Awareness of one's own imperfections and the effort to struggle against them? Such virtues are not popular anywhere in America today, but how desperately we need them! How desperately we need men and women who honor such qualities of the spirit if society is to be healed and the church restored to a place of leadership and respect!

Why are self-discipline and self-control important? Well, God never promised that the world would be a rose garden, and if we are going to be the hardened soldiers of the cross who won't turn tail and flee when the battle for truth gets costly, and if we're going to be of any use to God in fashioning a better world, then we can't waste our lives being spiritual couch potatoes who never learn what it means to say "no" to self and to the self's craven needs.

There is, fourthly, an emphasis on serving God in the world. Highes Old writes of the profound difference the Reformation made in the understanding of spirituality.

> For centuries spirituality had been cloistered. Christian life had meant to separate oneself from the world and enter a religious community.

It was there, in the convent or monastery, that medieval spirituality flourished. It was at its very heart a celibate, ascetic, and penitential devotion. With the Reformation the whole focus of the Christian life changed. Rather than separating themselves from human society, Christians began to think of devotion in terms of living out everyday life according to God's will. For Protestants spirituality became a matter of how one lived the Christian life with the family, out in the fields, in the workshop, in the kitchen, or at one's trade.[6]

Many years ago I tried to correct a popular idea about "church work" that is only half true. For most of us "church work" is only what we do here in this building on 214 Mountain Avenue, S. W., or what we do to support what goes on in this building. This idea is only partially correct. In terms of Reformed spirituality, "churchwork" is not only what we do inside these four walls, but what we do out in the world as representatives of the church. So, in preparation for a sermon I hoped would convert everyone's thinking, I asked all the members of the church to return a questionnaire listing not only their employment but the volunteer agencies in the community which they served. Then on the Sunday when I preached my masterpiece, there was an insert in the bulletin listing the things Second Presbyterians were doing in the world. "This," I said, "is our 'work of the church!'" I'd like to think our Protestant forebears were saying, "Well done, Mr. Klein!"

Reformed spirituality is about private prayer and personal Bible study and the solitary struggle of the soul, but it is also about working out our salvation in the world, making the world a better place for the common good. Reformed spirituality wants you to be concerned about the salvation of your soul, but about "the glory of God more than the salvation of one's own soul."[7]

Why is it important that we experience God's presence in the things we do in the world? Well, if God is serious about restoring a fallen world to the glory of creation, and if he calls us to be his faithful servants in transforming the world, then we're not likely to be of much use to him or to the world if our only interest is the enjoyment of spiritual experiences and the preparing of our little souls for heaven.

There are other qualities of Reformed/Presbyterian spirituality, but these, it seems to me, are especially important today. In a secular world where the Lord's Day is ignored, it is important for us to celebrate our Lord's resurrection each week as we come together to draw hope and courage from the Word of God. In a secular world where the multiplication of factual information results in a decline of wisdom, it is important for us to think

"Christianly," to be "wise as serpents," to use Jesus' terminology. In a secular world where everyone is looking for pleasure and the easy way, it is important for us to nurture those qualities of honesty and self-discipline and self-control, those qualities of the spirit that produce men and women with the moral stamina to fight the good fight of faith. In a secular world where everyone thinks that the spiritual life is the life of privatism and escape from the world, it is important for us to remember that God has called us to be his servants in the world.

I came across an article that asked a probing question that disturbs me and should disturb you. Where, it asked, are you Presbyterians and what are you doing when the world so desperately needs men and women of such stature?

16

The Promise of Christmas
John 1:14–18; Romans 8:11

AND THE WORD BECAME FLESH AND DWELT AMONG us, full of grace and truth; we have beheld his glory, glory as of the only Son from the Father. (John bore witness to him, and cried, "This is he of whom I said, 'He who comes after me ranks before me, for he was before me.'") And from his fulness we have all received, grace upon grace. For the law was given through Moses; grace and truth came through Jesus Christ. No one has ever seen God; the only Son, who is in the bosom of the Father, he has made him known.

John 1:14–18

If the Spirit of him who raised Jesus from the dead dwells in you, he who raised Christ Jesus from the dead will give life to your mortal bodies also through his Spirit which dwells in you.

Romans 8:11

For most of us, Christmas is the best time of the year. So at the risk of being "a Scrooge in clerical garb" I will toss some cold water on the typical fascination with Christmas. In the early church the great Christian holidays were Good Friday, Easter and Pentecost—never Christmas. These were the best times of the year. In fact, not until the fifth century did the church begin observing Jesus' birth.

Why was the early church slow in doing this? Part of it was resistance to pagan practices. Back then, before Hallmark cornered the market on birthday cards, birthday celebrations were reserved for kings and queens and other worthy notables. In fact, in the third century one church leader vigorously objected to any observance of Christ's birthday for this very reason. Shall we treat him "as if he were king Pharaoh?" he asked.

Strong resistance also came from the church's desire to be faithful to the New Testament. The disciples didn't run into the world shouting "Christ is born!" but "Christ is risen!" It was this news that turned lives around. In fact, in the entire New Testament only 125 verses are given to the story of Jesus' birth. And they occur only in Matthew and Luke. Mark, who wrote the earliest account of the gospel, makes no mention of it, but gives almost half of his telling of the story of Jesus to his final week, the week of his crucifixion and resurrection. Nor does Paul make any mention of Jesus' birth. For him also the wonder and mystery of Jesus are focused on his crucifixion and resurrection.

So what does it say about us that, unlike the early Christians, we call Christmas the best time of the year? Does it mean we understand better than they the mystery of Christ or the purpose of God? Or could it be that our enchantment with his birth means that we've forgotten the essential message of the gospel, that we'd rather have a baby to "coo" over than a Man whose love and truth are hard as flint? What do you think?

The good news of Christmas that can turn even our lives around doesn't have to do with babies or with innocence. No, the good news of Christmas is an affirmation about God that is grounded in the cross and resurrection. It is that affirmation, and nothing else, that gives importance to the birth of Jesus. If God had not raised him from death, we'd not be celebrating his birth. We wouldn't even know he ever walked this earth. So from cradle to empty tomb the story of Jesus is about the ultimate mystery we call God "who was in Christ reconciling the world to himself."[1]

"The Word (the most intimate entreaty of God's inmost Being) became flesh and dwelt among us, full of grace and truth." *The Word became flesh.* Can you, will you open your hearts to the unspeakable wonder of these four words?

Before all else these words are about God. So much does the hidden God of creation and history love us that he came down into our world to seek us out in that incomparable Man, Jesus.

The world gives no evidence of such love. It is not at all obvious that God has interest in us. Most of us live so comfortably it never occurs to us that the universe appears to be totally indifferent. Science finds no evidence that human life has ultimate value or that the cosmos is kind and loving. Even for some Christians God remains distant and remote, dwelling in heaven above, contemplating his own inscrutable thoughts, far removed from our chaotic world. For them God is the C.E.O. in his heavenly office who sends down memos from time to time, but who'd never risk soiling his

Brooks Brothers suit by venturing down into the basement where the sewer is backed up and everything's a stinking mess. Or they picture him as a cosmic puppeteer. When history reaches an impasse, he pulls strings that make us dance to his tune or he opens this floodgate and closes another to alter the flow of history. He will cheer us on in our struggle against ignorance and evil; he may even shed a tear or two when tragedy befalls us, but to believe that God cares deeply for each of us is a bold affirmation flung in the face of reality as most of us know it.

And if we can believe he really cares about us poor human creatures, it stretches our faith even more to believe the lengths to which he'll go in his love for the likes of us. I mean, if instead of always being romantic about the nobility of man and the upward progress of history, we looked at reality through the eyes of Bosnian children or Palestinian widows or the descendants of Holocaust survivors or the parents of children kidnapped and murdered by prison parolees; indeed, if we looked honestly at the quiet rage and potential for violence smoldering within us, hidden beneath a thin veneer of civic decency, we'd marvel that God doesn't crush us like loathsome insects. Certainly the natural world would be better off if it didn't have us burdening the earth with over-population or smearing it with our toxic waste.

Look all of this square in the face and it is nothing less than the miracle of miracles that God should send his beloved Son to redeem us. And he doesn't even wait for us to become likeable, grateful, and obedient children before he will love us. He comes down into the deepest reaches of our lives even as we flee from his loving embrace.

How deeply does God enter our lives? As deeply as a baby born in a cold, dirty, germ-filled stable without light and without water to wash the blood from his naked little body. As deeply as a man stretched out on a Roman cross as the flies swarmed on his dried blood and the scorching sun swelled his tongue and cracked his lips. Because of Jesus Christ we dare to believe there is no human situation beyond the reach of his love, that there is no one so low and despairing that she cannot look at him and call him, "my brother." God is that kind of God. He is the God who comes seeking us in our sinfulness and unbelief, refusing to give up on us even if we slap away his outstretched arms; even if we lynch his beloved Son.

If Christmas means anything, in fact, if Good Friday and Easter and Pentecost mean anything, it all means that God has come into the joy and hell of our human existence to give us a new beginning again and again whenever we turn to him in hope and love. This is the good news of Christmas, of the Word become flesh, that God is with us in life and in death, and that he does not give up on us or his creation.

And now the other half of the text's meaning. If the affirmation that the "Word became flesh" tells us who God is, it also tells who we are, or at least it gives the promise of our lives. If it is true that God's only begotten Son lived a totally sinless life in human flesh, then no longer can we excuse our repeated failings with the cavalier comment that we're only human. So was he. He is proof that our human flesh has the promise of Christlikeness. It means that you and I have the potential for such greatness, such magnificence, that no one less than the Son of God can be the measure of it. Irenaeus, the great second-century theologian was wont to ask, "For what purpose did Christ come down from heaven?" His answer: "Christ became man that we might be made divine." Who else has such dreams and hopes for you and me except the God and Father of our Lord Jesus Christ?

Is this an illusion? Are we too sinful for such dreams? Listen to St. Augustine! "Every man, from the commencement of his faith, becomes a Christian, by the same grace by which that Man Jesus from his formation, became Christ." The same Spirit of God who dwelt in Jesus Christ, who made him who he was and who raised him from the dead—that same Spirit dwells in us if we have given our miserable little lives over to Jesus Christ in faith and hope. Have you? Will you? For "if the Spirit of him who raised Jesus from the dead dwells in you, he who raised Christ Jesus from the dead will give life to your mortal bodies also."

This is why we will not believe the gospel. It calls us to be greater than we want to be. And that's saying something, given our chronic egotism. We keep trying to settle for the world's paltry definitions of greatness, but the gospel keeps disturbing us. It keeps saying "no" to our petty little accomplishments, and it keeps calling us to an excellence so magnificent that it will take an eternity to realize it. This is why we resist the call of Christ, and this is why we make of Christmas little more than a celebration of babies and innocence and motherhood and gift-giving, because that Man who was born in Bethlehem of Judea in the days of Herod the king, keeps shattering our dinky little dreams and our trifling little goals. And in my better moments, which steal upon me far too seldom, I know in my heart of hearts that I would rather the judgment of God knock me flat for refusing the promise of my baptism than have the flattering gods of this world smile on my tawdry, mediocre life.

How sweet it is to know that God loves the likes of us, loves us enough to send his only Son to die for us. It's this other part of the story that I keep trying to ignore, the part that says I can be far better than I am, the part that says, "If the Spirit that made Christ who he was and raised him from the

93

dead dwells in you," then you should be better than you are. And that means being more Christlike, being more willing to forgive, less driven to talk about things I dislike about others, less concerned with my success, my material comforts, having my way, less quick to blame others when things go wrong and more eager to give credit to others when things go right, more determined never to make anyone feel inferior or unimportant. This is the part I'd rather ignore, and so do you.

There was a university student who sometimes attended worship. Leaving church one day he said to the minister, "I'm beginning to think the gospel is true, and I wish it weren't!" *I wish it weren't!* I know what he means. If only Jesus had remained a sweet, innocent baby! After all, how we flatter ourselves when we hold babies in our arms and marvel at God's gifts of love. (How lovely we are to be moved by babies!) But he had to go and become that towering Man who gives us no peace until we let him fashion us into the perfect children of God we are meant to be.

"And the Word became flesh and dwelt among us, full of grace and truth" not only to assure us that God is with us and for us, but also to assure us that we are destined for greatness. And I'll tell you, once you know the claim he has on you, you can't remain the same; you have to do something, even if it's no more than wishing it weren't true and trying your best to forget that you ever knew him. But forgetting him is never easy. Do you sometimes wish you could? "Maybe the first bit of real evidence you'll ever have that you've met him is just this"[2] disquieting knowledge that now you have been called to greatness.

In this Jesus we have met the One who summons us to an impossible greatness, but when he speaks, we dare to believe he can make it happen.

17

Understanding the Gospel

Matthew 13:1–12; 1 Corinthians 2:14–16

RECENTLY I WAS LOOKING THROUGH SOME OLD CHURCH bulletins. Much to my surprise I found that the second sermon I preached from this pulpit was on the parable of the soils. It was Sunday, June 23, 1968. That parable is our scripture lesson for the morning.

If this parable teaches anything, it is that our ability to hear and understand the gospel depends on the kind of person we are. Intelligence or lack of it counts for very little where the mystery of God is concerned. So if the story of God's love in Jesus Christ makes no deep impression on us or fails to stir our dull hearts, if it does not move us to ask with trembling lips, "Who am I, Lord?" then the problem may well be with us and not the gospel. Listen then to the parable as Matthew tells it.

That same day Jesus went out of the house and sat beside the sea. And great crowds gathered about him, so that he got into a boat and sat there; and the whole crowd stood on the beach. And he told them many things in parables saying: "A sower went out to sow. And as he sowed, some seeds fell along the path, and the birds came and devoured them. Other seeds fell on rocky ground, where they had not much soil, and immediately they sprang up, since they had no depth of soil, but when the sun rose they were scorched; and since they had no root they withered away. Other seeds fell upon thorns, and the thorns grew up and choked them. Other seeds fell on good soil and brought forth grain, some a hundredfold, some sixty, some thirty. He who has ears, let him hear."

Then the disciples came and said to him, "Why do you speak to them in parables?" And he answered them, "To you it has been given to know the secrets of the kingdom of heaven, but to them it has not been given. For to him who has will more be given, and he will have abundance; but from him who has not, even what he has will be taken away."

Matthew 13:1–12

I have another text on this theme of spiritual discernment. It's from one of Paul's letters to the church at Corinth.

The unspiritual man does not receive the gifts of the Spirit of God, for they are folly to him, and he is not able to understand them because they are spiritually discerned. The spiritual man judges all things, but is himself to be judged by no one. "For who has known the mind of the Lord so as to instruct him?" But we have the mind of Christ.

1 Corinthians 2:14–16

Some suggest that if the church wants to reverse declining membership rolls and start growing again, it needs to engage a good advertising agency. Not only can a good ad agency tell you what modern people want from religion; it can also tell you how to package your message in simple terms so everyone can understand it and like what is heard.

But would it be the gospel they'd understand and like? Certainly a simple, catchy ad can sell cars or win votes. It can even persuade people to join a good organization or support a good cause. But interpret the gospel? Were we to put our future in the hands of advertisers, the churches would thrive but Christianity would die. After all, even people who saw Jesus in the flesh and who heard him speak could hardly make heads or tails of what he was about. In fact, when Jesus explained his use of parables it seems as if he wanted his message to be ambiguous and hard to comprehend in order to discourage casual seekers who had no stomach for the service of God and his kingdom.

Easy to understand? What if it is true that we must come in off the street, wash off the grime of the world's assumptions and priorities, and enter the strange universe of the Bible if we hope to understand! And what if something deep, deep within us has to be changed before we can understand even the ABCs of the gospel! The seed of the gospel can grow only in soil that is fertile and receptive.[1]

Blaise Pascal, seventh-century genius, was profoundly gifted in both mathematics and theology. In a memorable treatise, closely akin to Jesus' parable of the soils, he argued that we all belong to one of three orders of

96

being or spiritual types. We may belong to the order of the body, or to the order of the intellect, or to the order of the heart which is the highest and most spiritual of all. And each order, each type, has its own major concerns which make it blind and deaf to the concerns of the higher orders. Only people who belong to the order of the heart, he said, can truly fathom the gospel and give themselves to it.[2]

Do you know the order to which you belong; the order that dictates your values, your priorities, your dreams?

The order of the body, said Pascal, is not to be confused simply with sensuality: with food and drink and sex and physical beauty and bodily comforts, though that is certainly part of it. No, he said, people of the order of the body believe their ultimate well-being can be gained and secured only through riches and power. With riches and power they can walk with an air of superiority, manipulate others with money or threats, and protect themselves from the vicissitudes of life which are always a threat to the poor and the weak. What is more, while people of the body may feel occasional twinges of pity for the weak and defenseless, at Thanksgiving or Christmas, for example, they are incapable of empathy for the fearful and fragile existence of the weak. To those who live on the fringes, they always preach the same sermon: "You can be just like me if you only try!"

People of the order of the body have no capacity for appreciating beauty for its own sake or truth for its own sake as do people of the intellect. Such things have value only as status symbols or as commodities to be sold for profit or used to obtain research grants.

And, of course, people of the order of the body can be very religious. But for them, God's primary responsibility is to reward them with health, wealth and happiness for their pious adulations. If they're looking for a church their first question is whether the social status of its members is sufficiently impressive, or whether its sermons and programs are to their unconverted tastes, never the divine truth it proclaims and tries to live by, or its service to others.

It is not surprising, then, that people of the order of the body were immediately attracted to Jesus. After all, he healed the sick, fed the hungry, told clever little stories, and exposed the pretensions of the pompous. But at the first mention of self-denial or of taking up even the tiniest cross to follow him, they fled like rats from a sinking ship. People of the order of the body are incapable of understanding what the gospel is really about, even though they can be very religious.

People of the order of the intellect, says Pascal, give themselves to the life of the mind. Their greatest joy is the pursuit of truth, regardless of

97

whether it makes them rich or famous or powerful. Are there any pure intellectuals left in our world? In a culture that puts a dollar sign on everything, what good is it to be a genius if it doesn't make you rich and powerful and famous?

✓ Nonetheless, people of the order of the intellect, when they are true to their type, love knowledge for its own sake. But they are as blind to the mysteries of the heart as people of the order of the body are blind to the value of truth for its own sake. For example, the late Rollo May, the great psychiatrist, once said of his New York practice that each day brilliant clients came through his office who could talk for hours on end about the intellectual aspects of their problems, but who seemed incapable of exposing their vulnerabilities and weaknesses, incapable of seeing any personal responsibility for the mess they'd made of life, and incapable of giving themselves to another in trusting love.

And when it comes to religion, people of the order of the intellect seem incapable of reaching out to God in humble faith. It's as if they set up their own little minds as the supreme arbiter of truth, and then expect God to shape up and conform to their assumptions and to their self-styled omniscience if he wants them to give him serious attention. And if they deign to talk about religion at all, it must be on the safe theoretical level—safe because on that level no commitment of the heart and will is required. They prefer discussion and dialogue rather than sermons so they can use their clever sophistries to fend off the Word of God with its dreadful claims. And how smug they feel if they can walk away triumphantly after having put down a humble believer with their arcane knowledge of philosophy or science or history. Their love of knowledge, instead of making them more receptive to the gift of faith, seems to render them blind and deaf to the quiet and non-coercive love of God.

People of the order of the heart, on the other hand, are given the grace to love God for his own sake, to find in Jesus Christ such beauty and love that their hearts are hushed in adoring silence, and to embark with hope and joy on a lifelong pilgrimage that will not let them rest till they rest in his presence. People of the heart do not scorn the things of the body that give happiness and pleasure, but neither are they driven by lust for power or riches. They can survive the loss of worldly goods and still keep opening their hearts to the future. And they are secure enough in the grace of God to understand the anger and the fear of the weak who live on the edge of life and have so little. Nor do they scorn the gifts of the mind. They relish digging deeper and deeper into the treasure-trove of knowledge, because they are discovering that the more they know, the greater is their awareness of the awesome mystery of God.

Jesus is the Lord of the heart and the pioneer and perfecter of the order of the heart.

> "Without wealth or any outward show of knowledge," wrote Pascal, "Jesus has his own order of holiness. He made no discoveries; he did not reign, but he was humble, patient, thrice holy to God, terrible to devils, and without sin."[3]

Commenting on these words of Pascal, Diogenes Allen writes: "Jesus does not have the greatness of the order of the body, as does Alexander the Great" or the oil-rich sheiks of Saudi Arabia; "nor does he have the greatness of the order of the intellect, as does Einstein. According to Pascal, Jesus' greatness is his humility."[4] Is not this the supreme virtue, the one virtue which allows God to shine through one's life? "Jesus did not measure himself by the cultural standards of his day, as did some others, who scoffed at the fact that he was a carpenter (Mark 6:3), nor did he measure himself by the greatness of the order of the intellect (his education was that which could be gained at the local synagogue school)."[5] And yet his simple, penetrating words of truth could cut clean through the pretensions of the wise and erudite and leave them mumbling in their beards.

If then, the only truly authentic human being ever to walk this earth lived not by the order of the body or the order of the intellect, but by the order of the heart that loves God, and in loving God, is free to love the world, why do we insist on seeking our well-being in those things that fall so far short of his greatness; things that not only fall far short of his greatness but render us blind and deaf to the very riches of God he brings to us?

Ludwig Wittgenstein, the founder of the modern school of philosophy called "Logical Positivism," has written that "in religion every level of devoutness must have its appropriate form of expression which has no sense at a lower level. This doctrine, which means something at a higher level, is null and void for someone who is still at the lower level."[6]

If we are primarily people of the order of the body or people of the order of the intellect, then the order of the heart where Jesus lived and to which he calls us can make no sense. And it is not more knowledge or clearer thinking we must have, but a reordering of our whole understanding of life. Only when the grace of God shatters the blindness and deafness of our souls and lifts us up into his embrace in Jesus Christ—only then can we begin to know and understand. Are we willing to let him do this?

Jesus said that only the pure in heart can see God. It is also true that only the pure in heart can begin to understand the gospel. But how are hearts purified? This is grist for another sermon, but let me say two things briefly.

First, Pascal went on to say that hearts are purified as we accept the judgments of God upon our proud and selfish ways and begin to want what he wants and to love what he loves. But we refuse to receive the judgments of God in penitence and faith. Instead, we react in anger and defensiveness, blaming everyone else for whatever is wrong: our genetic history, our domineering parents, the spouse God gave us, our ungrateful children, society, the government, the stupidities of former generations, the signs of the Zodiac, aliens from outer space. So our hearts are not purified, and our souls remain blind and deaf to the evils in us that render us insensitive to the gospel.

Secondly, Pascal said our hearts are purified through pain and suffering that clears the eyes of the soul and invites us to understand how helpless and vulnerable we are in this world. But we do not receive the lessons of suffering. Instead, we react with self-pity and anger, blaming God. So our hearts are not purified, and our souls remain blind and deaf to our need for the gospel.

Does this mean that if we refuse the tasks of spiritual growth we are forever doomed to be corrupt of heart and thus incapable of understanding the gospel? No, not unless we defiantly harden our hearts against the tiny flashes of goodness and love that sometimes shine in our darkness. Not unless, proud of our sneering cleverness, we call evil good, and good evil, thus sinning against whatever decency may remain in our poor souls.

God knows the hearts where he is welcome, if it is only a murmur of a whisper that speaks his name in hope. So if some capacity to feel the pull of pure goodness, and the beauty of Jesus Christ, and the non-coercive power of his cross remain in us, then no matter how stubbornly we resist the heavy/light tasks of spiritual growth there is still a corner of fertile soil where the seed of the gospel can take root. For God does not give up on us; no, not even if we make our bed in hell. And who knows, perhaps it will take the dark, lonely trauma of death to open our eyes and unstop our ears to that love God has been waiting so long to give. Then at last we will know and understand, and I rather suspect we will look back and curse the wasted years when we could have known such love, such hope, such joy.

It is the first Sunday of Advent. What are you doing to make ready your cluttered, hardened soul for the quiet coming of the Lord?

18

A Colony of Heaven

Matthew 18:20; John 13:34–35; Philippians 3:20–4:1

THE *NEW YORK TIMES* MENTIONED A SPEECH WHICH columnist Georgie Anne Geyer gave at Northwestern University in which she speaks of the forces of division.

The problem for the United States in your lifetime, will . . . be related to the problems we see in theYugoslavias, the Tajiksttans, and . . . the Russias of our world. It is the problem of national and cultural disintegration. For in our own way we are allowing organizers, activists, and ambition-ridden political putative leaders to divide this country in much the same way that Yugoslavia has been deliberately divided since 1987.[1]

Reporting on her speech, Martin Marty asks, "Where is religion in all of this?"[2] Does religion feed the fires of hate that divide people? If so, can the church repent, change, and become a positive force, bringing people together instead of setting them against one another? With this question in mind, hear the Word of God!

Jesus said, "Where two or three are gathered in my name, there am I in the midst of them."

Matthew 18:20

Jesus said, "A new commandment I give to you, that you love one another; even as I have loved you, that you also love one another. By this all men will know that you are my disciples, if you have love for one another."

John 13:34–35

Paul wrote, "Well then my brothers, rejoice in the Lord. For we are a colony of heaven, and we wait for the Savior who will transform the body that belongs to our low estate till it resembles the body of his glory, by the same power that enables him to make everything subject to himself. So then, my brothers, for whom I cherish love and longing, my joy and my crown, this is how you must stand firm in the Lord, O my beloved."

Philippians 3:20–4:1 (MOFFATT)

I was a child of the Great Depression. What I remember from my childhood is playing cowboys and Indians, walking on Sunday afternoons with my father in the woods and open fields that surrounded our home in suburban Atlanta, building tree houses, and an occasional Saturday matinee to see "Our Gang" or "Hopalong Cassidy." I was largely unaware of world events. I know now, however, that there were a few voices warning us of the dark storm clouds gathering in Europe. But mostly those voices were ignored. Everyone preferred to sing "Happy Days Are Here Again" and to hear the always-popular political promises of prosperity and happiness just around the corner. And then my childhood world suddenly went up in flames with the attack on Pearl Harbor on December 7, 1941.

Are we poor human creatures fated forever to close our eyes to storm clouds that fill the horizon?

I think about what is happening right now. Are we blithely whistling in the dark, refusing to take seriously the daily signs that our world of values and the civilization built upon those values is crumbling like a damp wall of rotting bricks? The beating of Rodney King by the police in Los Angeles and the trials that satisfied no one, irreconcilable differences over social and personal values that divide our country into hostile camps, strident voices demanding to have their way no matter what the social cost, the numbing fear as we watch the increase of violence and the helplessness of government to curb it. All of this gives credence to Ms. Geyer's warning. And I wonder, are we like people in the thirties, unwilling or unable to take seriously the gathering storm?

Because we are Christians, another question is troublesome. Is the church part of the problem or part of the solution? And if, in God's grace, we can be part of the solution, what is it the church can do in a world coming apart? Well, this is the issue before us.

I really have but one thing to say, and that is this: The one and only thing we have to offer the world is simply to be the church. But what does this mean? The hundreds of denominations in America testify to the many different notions of the church's nature and purpose. And were I to ask you to jot down your answer I'd get as many different replies as there are people here this morning. So let me draw some images from the New Testament and at least offer a little of my understanding of what it means to be the church in these few remaining years of the twentieth century.

Our first text says that we are the church when Christ is in our midst. "Where two or three are gathered in my name (or in my spirit) there am I in the midst of them." If he is not present we are simply a religious club, not the church. The church is not a private club of like-minded people intent on doing good, nor a self-help group for folks hurt by the harsh realities of life, nor an association of people who are morally and spiritually superior. It is not even a society for the preservation of the great ideals for which Jesus lived. The living Christ must be present if a church is a church, so an unbelieving world can look at a particular church and say, "So this tells me something of the life Jesus lived when He was here on earth!"

A second text says that the church is a new community of men and women who love one another as Christ loves us. How does the song go? "They shall know we are Christians by our love!" Do you know any congregations an unbelieving world can look at and say, "Behold how these Christians love one another!" or "Never before have we seen such love in any of the communities of this world!?"

Our third text is from a letter from Paul. He calls the church "a colony of heaven." This is an apt metaphor, because "the church provides the setting in which Christians can practice their Christianity, freed from the hindrances of worldly social pressure, and supported by a community committed to the same Lord and the same way of life."[3] Do you know any congregations an unbelieving world can look at and say, "So this is a clue to the kind of community we can expect to find in heaven!"

Did you notice a common thread in all of these texts? One obvious thread is a Christ-like or heavenly presence. But a second thread is relational. The church is not a collection of isolated, autonomous individuals, but a new community of faith, hope, and love. None of these texts speak of correct beliefs or doctrines, none speaks of moral accomplishments, none speaks of humanitarian causes to change society, as important as all these are. None speaks of institutional wealth or size. In fact, Jesus' promise to be present if only two or three are gathered in his name makes a lie of our proud assumption that the church with the most members is somehow the best church. Each of these texts reminds us that being the church has first and foremost to do with our relationship with Jesus Christ and with each other. In fact, these texts suggest that you can't separate the two. If you don't love your fellow Christian whom you have seen, you can't love God whom you've never seen.[4]

For too long the church has been crippled by an individualism that ignores the essential relational aspect of Christianity. An excessive individualism has said, "My private relation with God is all that matters: my salvation, my private prayers, my moral improvement, my down payment on a condominium in heaven." Certainly these things are not to be ignored, but each is corrupted by the popular heresy that being a Christian is a private self-improvement program, a "do-it-yourself" project which renders the church and other Christians irrelevant or optional, depending on your personal preferences. Hasn't our individualism made popular that totally non-biblical idea that no one needs the church to be a Christian? So listen up! While being a Christian is profoundly personal and intimate, it is never ever a private, individual affair. Never!

If you want to see the tragedy of this excessive individualism in society, then look no farther than today's news: at corporate boards that will spare no expense for lawyers who can find loopholes in environmental laws and labor laws so they can go on doing business as usual, at mothers mourning over victims of America's gun-toting trash, or at the millions of children who have been alternatively abused and abandoned by fathers whose only interest is their own erotic pleasure. If you want to see the tragedy of this excessive individualism in the church, look at the easy conscience with which so-called Christians who get their feelings hurt or who can't have their way, withdraw to organize a new religious club and then have the audacity to call that club a church, the body of Christ.

Instead of being the new community of love, showing an unbelieving world the kind of community God intends, we have too often carried this devil's weak gruel of individualism into the church and baptized it with sacred dignity. No wonder the world and the church are no better than they are.

And yet there are congregations here and there which, in spite of their human failings, approximate this noble calling to be the church. Some of us have been shaped by them. But it's hard to believe such churches exist if you read most modern novels or watch television or listen to the cynical teachers of our youth. Sometimes I have the distinct feeling that the people who shape popular opinion have never seen a real church, have never known a true family of faith where people follow Jesus Christ with humility and joy, where people are loving and open and trusting, where people honestly confess their sins and strive to be better for Christ's sake, where petty differences are never allowed to dig chasms of alienation, where concern for the hopeless and the despairing is genuine, and where the historic truth of the gospel is honored. But such churches do exist, large and small, rich and poor, Catholic and Protestant, and some of us have found a taste of heaven within their sacred walls.

And it is my conviction that when the church is truly a colony of heaven, then its influence on an unbelieving world can and will be healing. Interesting, isn't it, how the early church, a helpless minority in the Roman world, without a single vote to cast, eventually changed accepted practices of Roman society: slavery and the abandonment of unwanted children, to give but two examples. And those early Christians did it simply by living a different kind of life within the church, so that men and women who remained slaves in society became brothers and sisters in the church, and so that children who often had no inherent worth in the world were baptized, loved, and nurtured in the church because Jesus Christ gave to little ones a new and previously unheard of dignity. The Roman world could not long continue as it was with such new and different communities of faith and love in its midst.

You know as well as I that the world is coming apart. Maybe the world is always coming apart. If we become serious about being the church, the new community of love, truth, and peace which Christ intends, a colony of heaven, will we really make a difference in this poor world of ours which is disintegrating before our very eyes? I can offer no proof that dedicated Christians and genuine colonies of heaven can save this world from self-destruction. But I can promise that if we dare to be the community of faith Christ wants us to be, if we have the courage to forge a life together unlike anything the world offers, if we are willing to commit ourselves to each other and to suffer loss so that this family of faith can shine like a beacon of hope in a darkening world, then whether or not the world falls apart we will have fulfilled our calling to be a colony of heaven. And if the world does come apart, future generations may look at us and say, "There were Christians in the land in that dark night, and for the sake of their faithfulness and the faithfulness of him who never failed us, we too will dare to be a pilgrim people."

19

The Sacred Limits
Others Pose for Us

Ephesians 4:22–32

LET ME BEGIN WITH A STATEMENT ABOUT GOOD AND evil. The evil we do is usually the result of our refusal to accept any limits to our self-worship and self-seeking. Good, on the other hand, comes to pass when we say "no" to self and honor the limits others pose for us, especially if that other is God. If this is true, then we cannot love unless we are free to do what is good, for love grows out of respect for the dignity and freedom of others.

In our text for the morning, Paul offers guidance to the Christians of Ephesus as they struggle to do what is good in the midst of a pagan society where it was just as easy to do evil as it is in ours. As you listen, notice how goodness has to do with honoring the dignity and freedom of others.

> Put off your old nature which belongs to your former manner of life and is corrupt through deceitful lusts, and be renewed in the spirit of your minds, and put on the new nature, created after the likeness of God in true righteousness and holiness. Therefore, putting away falsehood, let every one speak the truth with his neighbor, for we are members one of another. Be angry but do not sin; do not let the sun go down on your anger, and give no opportunity to the devil. Let the thief no longer steal, but rather let him labor, doing honest work with his hands, so that he may be able to give to those in need. Let no evil talk come out of your mouths, but only such as is good for edifying, as fits the occasion, that it may impart grace to those who hear. And do not grieve the Holy Spirit of God, in whom you were sealed for the day of redemption. Let all bitterness and wrath and anger and clamor and slander be put away from you, with all malice, and be kind to one another, tender-hearted, forgiving one another, as God in Christ forgave you.
>
> *Ephesians 4:22–32*

The Sacred Limits Others Pose for Us

Why does God create other people and give them to us? So we can love and be loved in return. When God saw Adam's loneliness he said, "It is not good that the man should be alone; I will make him a helper fit for him."[1] Does this ancient text suggest that even with God's companionship Adam's life was still incomplete and that God saw man's deep, deep need for others? God does not create us to live solitary, lonely, individual lives. In his infinite love He creates us for life together.

Let me now suggest a second reason why God surrounds our lives with others. He does it so we can learn goodness. Others pose limits to our idolatry of self. God surrounds us with other lives to put a check on our inordinate passion to have our own way.

In order to understand what this means we have to understand what Christianity means by sin. In classical Christianity, sin is not bad thoughts or bad deeds but a fundamental perversion at the very core of our being. Sin is a self turned in upon itself, a self that tries to be the center of the universe, a self that demands that everyone, including God, bow down to its needs and demands. Thus defined, sin is the basic form of idolatry, an idolatrous worship of one's own self with its needs, wants, and desires. I become the center of my universe, and in my sinfulness others are valued only for what they can do for me. And worst of all, even God is valued only for what he can do for me. This is how religion turns rancid and compounds our sinfulness. It attempts to capture God for our purposes.

So long as we imagine that the world revolves around us, we are incapable of authentic love and authentic goodness. What is more, in our sin we resent the limits others pose for us, and we refuse to let the existence of others restrain our determination to bend everyone and everything to our needs, wants, and desires. Now God's gift of others is no longer received with joy; others are now a threat to my god-almightiness, as I am to theirs. So one of the characters in Jean-Paul Sartre's play No Exit cries out: "Hell—is others."[2]

The ancient story in Genesis tells how the Fall radically altered the oneness and trust God intended for Adam and Eve. Fallen man now sees the other as a limit to his needs and wants, especially his lust. Dietrich Bonhoeffer wrote of this change with profound insight.

> Now the limit is no longer grace, holding man in the unity of his creaturely and free love; it is discord. Man and woman are divided. Man makes use of his share of the woman's body; more generally, one man makes use of his right to the other and puts forward his claim to the possession of the other, thereby denying and destroying the other

person's creatureliness. This avid passion of man for the other person first comes to expression in sexuality. The sexuality of man who has transgressed his limit is the refusal to recognize any limit whatever; it is the boundless passion to be without limit. Sexuality is the passionate hatred of every limit, it is arbitrariness to the highest degree, it is self-will.[3]

Let's go one step further. It is easy to do evil; it is hard to do good. How sweet it is to get what we want, to have our desires met, to have others do our bidding. We are exhilarated. The future is ours. Nothing can stop us. And if we use a few people and push some aside and destroy a few to get our way, that's their problem, not ours. Getting what we want is everything. So the hero in our American culture is the rugged individual who is self-reliant, answers to no one but himself, gets what he wants, and lets no thing and no one stand in his way. He or she is the very opposite of what Christianity defines as a good person. And yet popular American religion hardly understands what this means. Could this be one reason why the church has little influence as we lay waste to the environment? Could this be one reason why our society is torn asunder and is incapable of forging a sense of community in spite of American religiosity?

It is God's intention that we learn goodness as we come up against the limits posed by others: by family members, neighbors, people with whom we work, members of the church, voting blocks across town. If God's will were done "on earth as it is in heaven," being confronted by these limits would nudge us to face up to our idolatry of self and our inordinate self-seeking. Are you surprised that such facing up to these limits is what one philosophical theologian of note calls the judgment of God?[4]

So we fall in love because the other meets our needs; our wants and desires are served by this person. But what do we do if the needs and freedom of the other place a limit on our needs, desires, and wants? Well, we can do one of two things. We can accept the limitation, receive it as the gracious judgment of God saving us from our own god-almightiness, rein in our selfishness, learn that we are mere mortals and not gods, and thus grow in our capacity for goodness and love. Or we can see those limits as a deadly threat to our god-almightiness giving us license to do physical or spiritual violence to this despicable person who resists us, cast him or her aside as something useless, look for another creature who will worship us and let us have our way, and thus sink deeper into the hell of our isolated selves. Recognizing this, someone has advised that we do not marry because of love; we marry so we can learn how to love.

Think of all the evils that we base creatures inflict upon others! Don't they arise from hearts that refuse to acknowledge that God alone is God and that others are to be honored and loved, not used?

It is proof of the grace of God in this world that many people profit by the sacred limits of others. They learn to say "no" to self, learn to do good by honoring the freedom and dignity of others, and thereby learn to open their hearts to the ultimate mystery who is God.

But some never learn. Diogenes Allen writes that "the great temptation of power and wealth is to override whatever limits our desires and wishes. Power and wealth give us the means to do so."[5] If I have physical power or military power or political power or legal power or the power of a strong personality, I can ride roughshod over others to achieve whatever I want. And such power becomes especially dangerous if I'm convinced that what I want is good for everyone.

The same is true of wealth. It affords me endless opportunities to run away from facing up to myself. If my neighbors oppose what I want, I either buy them out or go somewhere else where I can have my way. Likewise, with sufficient wealth I can buy the friends I want or the politicians I want or the lawyers I want or the preachers I want. The poor have no such options.

These are the raw uses of power and wealth, but there are more subtle forms of power that subdue others. I can use intellectual power to beat my opponent into submission, compel him to agree with me or be branded an idiot. Or what about the abuse of moral and spiritual power? I've known preachers and Sunday school teachers and righteous parents who used their spiritual authority to mow down anyone who disagreed with them. They would not relent till they forced their idea of God's will on everyone. Or what about the subtle power of those who pride themselves in their weakness, helplessness, and poverty, or the gross injustices they've suffered? We all know what it is to be manipulated by those who whine about how oppressed they are and how much they are to be pitied. "Poor little me, look how I've been victimized!" And once they've hooked you with guilt, they can often have their way.

It is true of everyone: Either we learn the gracious truth God seeks to teach us when we come up against limits, or we insist on having our way and sink deeper into the solitary hell of our own god-almightiness.

What is life teaching you about God and others and your own self?

Let's go back now to the pastoral guidance Paul offered the Christians of Ephesus. But before I say anything else, let me remind you that those Ephesian Christians had become new and different men and women because they had given their lives to Jesus Christ. Their morality was not a do-it-yourself project. With Jesus Christ they had crucified their old sinful selves and were beginning to grow new selves—selves that had enthroned God at the center of life. If that's clear, we can go on with Paul's counsel.

Paul says, "Putting away falsehood, let everyone speak the truth with his neighbor." Why? Not because truth-telling makes me an honorable gentleman so I can better get people to listen to me, but because "we are members one of another" and telling the truth in love builds trust, without which there can be no true community. Paul says, "Be angry, but do not let the sun go down on your anger," which I take to mean that it's normal to have angry feelings, but you'd better not let them become the master of your behavior. Why? Not because controlling anger wins me brownie points with God, but because it keeps me from violating others. There must have been some former thieves in the church at Ephesus because Paul says, "Let the thief no longer steal, but rather let him labor, doing honest work with his hands." Why? Not because the converted thief can brag about what a good Christian he has become, but in order not to violate another's property. And more than that, "so he may be able to give to those in need." Paul says, "Let no evil talk come out of your mouths." Was he talking about "gossip" which he elsewhere ranks with "murder" and "hatred of God?"[6] Why refrain from "evil talk?" Not because it will improve my public image, but because "it may impart grace to those who hear."

The truth should be clear. To be a Christian is to accept as a gift from God, not only the people with whom he surrounds our poor, lonely lives, but the limits their very existence poses for the sin in us which always wants to be free to have its own way.

Can you be such a Christian? Do you want to be such a Christian? If so, let us join in the prayer of Thomas a Kempis!

> O merciful Lord, who hast made of one blood and redeemed by one ransom all nations of men, let me never harden my heart against any that partake of the same nature and redemption with me, but grant me an universal charity towards all men. Give me, O Father of compassion, such tenderness and meltingness of heart that I may be deeply affected with all the miseries and calamities outward or inward of my brethren, and diligently keep them in love. Grant that I may not only seek my own things, but also the things of others. O that this mind may be in us all, which was in the Lord Jesus, that we may love as brethren, be pitiful and courteous, and endeavor heartily and vigorously to keep the unity of the Spirit in the bond of peace, and the God of grace, mercy, and peace be with us all. Amen.

20

The Influence of
Noble Human Beings
Philippians 2:19–30

D O YOU KNOW SOMEONE YOU CAN TRULY HONOR AND respect? If you're a Christian, that will significantly limit the number of people worthy of it. Just because someone is rich or famous or powerful; just because someone shares your political views or religious views does not make her worthy of honor. One thing, and one thing alone, makes one worthy: something about that person's life must remind you of Jesus Christ. Blessed are you if you know such noble men and women, for if you truly honor them, you will grow in the likeness of the Christ they serve. Listen as Paul tells of two such servants of Christ whom he knew and loved!

I hope in the Lord Jesus to send Timothy to you soon, so that I may be cheered by news of you. I have no one like him, who will be genuinely anxious for your welfare. (There are others who pose as servants of Christ who) look after their own interests, not those of Jesus Christ. But Timothy's worth you know, how as a son with a father he has served with me in the gospel. I hope therefore to send him just as soon as I see how it will go with me; and I trust in the Lord that shortly I myself shall come also.

I have thought it necessary to send to you Epaphroditus my brother and fellow worker and fellow soldier, and your messenger and minister to my need, for he has been longing for you all, and has been distressed because you heard that he was ill. Indeed he was ill, near to death. But God had mercy on him, and not only on him but on me also, lest I should have sorrow upon sorrow. I am the more eager to send him, therefore, that you may rejoice at seeing him again, and that I may be less anxious. So receive him in the Lord with all joy; and honor such men, for he nearly died for the work of Christ, risking his life to complete your service to me.

Philippians 2:19–30

We know very little about Timothy even though two New Testament books carry his name. It is enough simply to know that he had Paul's unqualified trust. If there were problems in a church, Paul sent him as his personal envoy, and whatever he said was to be received as the words of Paul himself. Do you know anyone you trust so completely that you would back up their words with your own sacred honor?

Of Epaphroditus we know only that he was a leader in the church at Philippi. So when the church heard that Paul was under arrest in a distant city, a love offering was taken. And who but Epaphroditus would they trust to deliver the gift and to represent their love for Paul? So when time came for him to return to Philippi, he may well have carried this letter from Paul to the Philippians. If so, he must have made it back because the letter survives. He dropped from history after that, and we never hear of him again, but he had made his mark because Paul respected him.

Little do we know of either of these noble Christians, but the fact that Paul respected them and urged decent people to honor them was a greater prize than the praise of kings. What kind of people do we honor?

I never heard of Orvil Dryfoos until James Reston of the *New York Times* wrote an editorial on his death. Listen to this tribute to a simple human being who must have been the kind of person all of us would wish to be.

The death of Orvil Dryfoos was blamed on 'heart failure' but that obviously could not have been the reason. Orv Dryfoos' heart never failed him or anybody else—ask the reporters on the *Times*. It was as steady as the stars—ask anybody in the company of his friends. It was as faithful as the tides—ask his beloved wife and family. No matter what the doctors say, they cannot blame his heart.

In the spiritual sense, his heart was not a failure, but his greatest success. He had room in it for every joy and everybody else's joy. This was the thing that set him apart—this warmness and purity of spirit, this considerateness, of his mother, whom he telephoned every day, of his wife and children, of his colleagues and competitors. And this uncorrupted heart, broken or no, is what is likely to be remembered about him.

112

He had his weaknesses, like all of us, but usually they sprang from the more amiable qualities of the human spirit. To hurt a colleague was an agony for him, and in this savage generation, when men decide, other men often get hurt. But he could make up his mind. He suffered, but he acted.

Perhaps the simplest thing to say about him—and I believe I speak for my colleagues in this—is that the more we knew him, the more we respected him. He was a gentleman. He was faithful to a noble tradition, to the family from which he came, and to the great family he joined and loved.

Let us then honor Orvil Dryfoos with remembrance rather than with tears. For his children will never be able to cry as much as he has made them laugh.[1]

Recently I spent a week doing nothing but reading. I was trying to put together a class I hope to teach this winter. The class will wrestle with the "why?" of suffering and evil.

One of the books I picked up had slept unread in my library for quite a number of years. It's about people who have suffered in various ways: debilitating sickness, the premature loss of a loved one, the ravages of war, political oppression, economic injustice, religious persecution, public vilification. Its title? *Creative Suffering, The Ripple of Hope.*[2] Here were men and women, a noble, blessed few who personify the human spirit at its best. Here were men and women who overcame pain and hatred and cruelty, and in the overcoming of it, reached heights of gentleness and goodness and love that shame us who are surrounded by comfort, and who whine over the slightest inconvenience. Here were men and women who stretch our vision of human life. I felt clean just to have met them on the printed page, for here were flesh-and-blood people in whom the Spirit of Christ is real. And I put the book down thinking, "If only there were more of us like that, what a different world this would be."

One of the authors was Alan Paton. Some of you will remember him for his best known book, *Cry, the Beloved Country*. In the midst of South Africa's racial hatred and despair he held high the torch of Christian concern and hope. And because of it he knew suffering. Of suffering he said, "if there is any answer to it, it is not in trying to find an intellectually satisfying answer to the unanswerable question, 'Why?' nor in the writing of books and articles, but only in a life."[3] Thus the book's title, *Creative Suffering, The Ripple*

113

of Hope, not a tidal wave of hope—most of us are not good enough or courageous enough or humble enough to rise above the evils that befall us so we can be swept along by greatness—only a ripple of hope that tugs at some awareness in all of us that there's a forgotten nobility deep within us.

I was struck by Alan Paton's faith that the only answer to suffering is in living through it and above it. But isn't that the secret of everything? Doesn't truth become real only in living it? Theories and philosophies and ideologies, yes, even theologies, no matter how noble sounding, are nothing but empty words unless they become flesh and blood in the concrete particularity of a life. Thus the transcendent "word became flesh and dwelt among us, full of grace and truth."[4] Would we have known this Word of God otherwise?

How sad that we live in a time when we must constantly ask of public figures if they really believe the noble phrases they speak so passionately or whether they are simply mouthing propaganda to manipulate us! Helmut Thielicke often spoke of the need for men and women whose lives are all of one piece, whose private lives and public lives are cut from the same piece of cloth. And it is the breakdown of this oneness of public image and private life that has spread the deadly virus of cynicism that cancels our trust in our leaders and our institutions. We feel betrayed by people who talk piously about prayer in public but are never on their knees behind closed doors. We feel betrayed by politicians who speak eloquently on the campaign trail about using tax dollars to care for the needy, but who give only nickels and dimes from their own pockets to feed hungry neighbors. We feel betrayed by teachers who wave the flag of academic freedom, but ban prospective teachers from their department if they're not politically correct.

No wonder it is easy to become cynical! Maybe the media are to blame. It creates seductive public images of entertainers, politicians, athletes, and religious leaders and we're gullible enough to believe in those images. Then we discover that the images we believed in are lies, that in real life our heroes are corrupt, mean-spirited, immoral. Who knew that O. J. Simpson was violent and abusive? In his public image he was portrayed as the great American hero. His public life and his private life were not cut from the same piece of cloth.

Are all public figures afflicted by this dichotomy? No wonder it is easy to become cynical!

Another cause for deep concern! The world hungers for people who rep-resent the best we poor mortals can be, but such heroes and heroines of the human spirit get no press. They are ridiculed, pushed aside, and ignored by a world that counts wealth and power and cleverness and efficiency and aggressiveness and athletic prowess and immediate self-gratification at any cost and the fleeting beauty of youth to be the *sine qua non* of human existence. In such a world, Madonna is exciting, Mother Teresa a bore. In such a world, Donald Trump is a hero, Billy Graham a misfit. It is a world that values knowledge without love, power without compassion; words without truth; and pleasure without responsibility.

Or look at the popular heroes of the radio waves and the television screens—the talk show hosts or the self-styled expert commentators on the state of society. They thrive by pandering to our fears, our prejudices, our hatreds, our greed, our ignorance, our intellectual laziness, our fascination with cruelty and lust, our need to see evil conspiracies behind every change, our delight in seeing leaders with whom we disagree vilified with half-truths. We listen to them and our vision is not lifted, our hearts are not rendered more generous, our faith is not deepened, our determination to be better than we are is not strengthened. Their world is narrow and cynical and self-serving; nothing about the world they represent makes us feel clean or renews our hope for that kingdom of love and peace God has promised. Tell me, do you think they kindle hope and goodness and love and peace, or do they tear down everyone and everything except their own god-almightiness?

They thrive because they appeal to the worst within us. And perhaps their greatest evil is that they seduce us into thinking that we are most noble and good when this worst within us is given free reign. And they grow rich calling "evil good and good evil, by representing darkness for light and light for darkness."[5] That is the work of evil *par excellence.*

But perhaps the thing that is most distressing and heart breaking to me is our lack of discernment. How can it be that we who profess to know Jesus Christ, can listen to all this rhetoric that breeds suspicion and hatred and pettiness of spirit, and cannot see that it is the very opposite of everything that he is. And even if their public utterances have the ring of conviction, that in itself does not make it truth. Christianity is not about ideas or abstract values or beliefs or political promises or public rhetoric. It is about life, about your life and my life. It is about lives in whom the Spirit of Christ is evident. It is about lives that enable us to venture forth from the cramped, little, fearful world in which most of us live into a fresh, bright world full of goodness and promise. It is about lives that have discovered that freedom and joy are not to be found in carefully protecting ourselves but in giving ourselves away with hope and trust. The truth of public utterance has validity only if it is of one piece with the concrete, particular life that utters it.

And the world is hungry for such people of simple goodness whose lives represent the best we can be. Are we ready to be such people?

115

For many, the saving power of Jesus Christ is unconvincing until they can see something of his presence in the lives of those who bear his name. We are indeed the hope of the world. We? Yes, even we, if we let the Spirit of Christ gentle our proud little lives. In fact, we are of such importance that Jesus said, "Whoever hears you hears me, and whoever rejects you rejects me, and whoever rejects me rejects Him who sent me."[6] And you think who you are makes no difference?

Believe in him and in what he calls you to be, and become better than this cynical world believes anyone can be. And do it for the sake of him who loved us and gave himself up for us.

21

A Visit to Flossenburg

Philippians 1:12–14, 20–21

I WANT YOU TO KNOW, BRETHREN, THAT WHAT HAS happened to me has really served to advance the gospel, so that it has become known throughout the whole praetorian guard and to all the rest that my imprisonment is for Christ; and most of the brethren have been made confident in the Lord because of my imprisonment, and are much more bold to speak the word of God without fear.

It is my eager expectation and hope that I shall not be at all ashamed, but that with full courage, now as always, Christ will be honored in my body, whether by life or by death. For to me to live is Christ, and to die is gain.

Philippians 1:12–14, 20–21

You return from a trip and friends want to hear the thing that impressed you most, but not overly much. If you can tell your story in fifty words or less, and if you can do it without color slides, you may avoid boring them to death. All I can promise this morning is that I have no color slides.

Recently Dot and I were part of the American Summer Institute sponsored each year by Princeton Theological Seminary. We spent two delightful weeks in the little resort village of Les Avants, Switzerland, and a third week in Regensburg, Germany.

I must tell of the view awaiting us each morning. From our fourth-floor balcony of the hotel in Les Avants, high in the Swiss mountains, we looked out over the resort city of Montreux far below, and across Lake Geneva to the French Alps glistening with snow in the far distance. Early in the morning the air is crisp and clear, but by mid-morning the sun warms the earth and clouds begin to hide those majestic peaks. I will not soon forget that view or the cow bells greeting the dawn.

I was deeply moved when we worshiped in the ancient Cathedral of St. Piere in Geneva, built over Roman ruins. The service was in French, and I couldn't understand a word of it, so I kept imagining what it must mean to the minister of that church to preach from John Calvin's pulpit Sunday after Sunday. I'd always dreamed of worshiping in that church. It finally happened.

There was another day, a steamy afternoon, when we climbed a well-beaten path, higher and higher, to an ancient church overlooking the town of Sion. The church dates to the eighth century. By special arrangement, the organist gave our seminar a brief recital on the world's oldest functioning pipe organ.

Our teachers were impressive: Marcus Barth, son of the famed Karl Barth; Edward Schweizer, renowned New Testament scholar from the University of Zurich; Eberhard Bethge, fellow student and prisoner with Dietrich Bonhoeffer; Renate Bethge, Bonhoeffer's niece; Paul Albrecht, economist, who spoke of the church's role in a new Europe that is emerging.

But the event that moved me unforgettably was a visit to the little town of Flossenburg in Bavaria, not far from the famous city of Nuremberg. I dare say you've never heard of Flossenburg. Nearby was a Nazi concentration camp, not as big or efficient or notorious as Dachau or Auschwitz or Treblinka or Buchenwald, but a labor camp hallowed by Christians because of the execution of one man on Monday morning, April 9, 1945.

When Albert Einstein fled Germany in the thirties and came to America, he spoke of the surprising ease with which Adolf Hitler bewitched the German people. Einstein said he'd expected the great German universities, temples to intellectual freedom, to resist; but they welcomed Hitler with open arms. He said he'd then expected business leaders and labor leaders to resist. But they too embraced Hitler's seductions. "The only real opposition came from a source I never expected," said Albert Einstein, "from the church." One of the principal leaders of that opposition was Dietrich Bonhoeffer. He was the man whose life was taken at Flossenburg on April 9, 1945. He was thirty-nine years old.

Dietrich Bonhoeffer was born in 1906, the son of an old aristocratic German family. There were eight children in all, each one unusually gifted. Dietrich's father was head of the department of psychiatry at the University of Berlin. It's reported he had little use for Sigmund Freud and his brand of psychotherapy. Dr. Bonhoeffer thought it indecent to have to dredge up for discussion unseemly things that ought to remain buried in the psyche.[1] Dietrich's mother, also from a very aristocratic family, would have shared her husband's feelings.

118

At age sixteen Dietrich decided to study theology. Thus was launched an academic carrier studded with brilliant achievements. Years later, when Karl Barth read Bonhoeffer's doctoral dissertation, *Sanctorum Communio*, he called it "a theological miracle." A year of study at Union Seminary in New York City gave him lifelong contacts with church leaders here in America. In 1931, he returned to Germany to begin teaching at the University of Berlin.

On January 30, 1933, Adolf Hitler was installed as Chancellor of the Third Reich. Two days later on February 1, Bonhoeffer delivered a radio address from Berlin warning that the adulations being given to the new Chancellor as the savior of Germany would lead to disastrous idolatry. You wonder how he had the insight at that early date to see what everyone else failed to see. Well, the authorities broke off his radio address before he was finished, and from that moment on his name was in the Gestapo files as an opponent of the new regime.

It soon became evident that the German church had sold her soul to Adolf Hitler. The national church adopted an Aryan clause stating that any one with Jewish blood or anyone married to a Jew could not hold ecclesiastical office. There was also a requirement that all ministers swear absolute allegiance to the Führer. But large numbers of ministers, Germany's finest, flatly refused and eventually withdrew from the national church to organize a free church. Dietrich was a leader in this new Confessing Church and was asked to organize an independent seminary to train ministers for this new church.

It was Bonhoeffer's hope that the Confessing Church would awaken the German people to their senses and lead them to resist. But the Confessing Church was slowly emasculated. Ministers who refused to swear allegiance to Hitler were drafted into the army, the Gestapo closed the seminary, and Bonhoeffer was forbidden to teach or to speak in public anywhere in Germany. So with the collapse of the Confessing Church, Dietrich Bonhoeffer was drawn into the plot to overthrow Hitler. He and his brother Klaus, a noted physicist who once taught at the University of Chicago, were brought into the plot through a brother-in-law, Hans von Dohnanyi, who'd been a high official in the German Supreme Court. The unsuccessful assassination attempt on Hitler's life on July 20, 1944, led to the discovery of documents implicating everyone involved in the resistance movement. Many were immediately executed; all were eventually imprisoned.

So on the evening of April 3, 1945, the Tuesday after Easter, Dietrich Bonhoeffer, together with members of the German General Staff and other high-ranking government officials who had opposed Hitler, were loaded into an army truck destined for Flossenburg in the Bavarian countryside.

The war was almost over at this point, but Hitler was determined to eradicate, at the last minute, the brightest and best of that generation. Such killing was senseless. But in his paranoia, some have suggested, he believed Germany had betrayed him, so Germany deserved no future. Thus he ordered the wasteful execution of that generation's best who might help lift Germany from the ashes of defeat.

One day our seminar boarded a private bus and rode about two hours from Regensburg to Flossenburg. On the way we passed the village of Schönberg. On an April day in 1944, the army trucks bearing Bonhoeffer and his prominent German compatriots stopped at Schonberg. The work camp at Flossenburg was overcrowded at the moment, so they were billeted in the schoolhouse at Schönberg. On Sunday, April 8, Bonhoeffer conducted a worship service in that little school house for his fellow prisoners. His meditation came from two verses of scripture, Isaiah 53:5: "With his wounds we are healed!" and 1 Peter 1:3: "Blessed be the God and Father of our Lord Jesus Christ! By his great mercy we have been born anew to a living hope through the resurrection of Jesus Christ from the dead."

That afternoon a black Mercedes came to the schoolhouse at Schönberg to take Bonhoeffer to Flossenburg. It was about an hour's drive. In the east they could hear the guns of the advancing Russian army; in the west the guns of the rapidly advancing American army. Our bus followed that route from Schönberg to Flossenburg. We passed the same fertile farmland, bathed in the sun, the same stately pines standing guard over the lush earth. I kept thinking of Paul's words written from prison to his friends at Philippi: "Most of the brethren have been made confident in the Lord because of my imprisonment." "For me to live is Christ, and to die is gain." We drove through the neat, quiet village of Flossenburg. The citizens of the village claim to have had no knowledge of the things that took place in the work camp nearby. I kept marveling at our human capacity for denial. And then the bus had stopped and we were there.

At dawn on a cold Bavarian Monday morning, April 9, 1945, Dietrich Bonhoeffer was stripped naked, marched to one end of the prison courtyard and hanged. Did the words of Job flash before his mind? "Naked came I from my mother's womb, and naked shall I return." A few days later Flossenburg was liberated by the American army. A marble plaque stands where the hangman's noose once swung. On it are the names of Pastor Dietrich Bonhoeffer; Admiral Wilhelm Canaris, head of German Military Intelligence; Major General Hans Oster, coordinator of the resistance movement, and the names of two others I cannot recall.

A Visit to Flossenburg

From that one remaining barracks where the plaque stands, we walked under trees that have grown up over ground where barracks once stood, as if to hide from heaven's eyes that place of loneliness, horror, and suffering. We walked past barbed wire that was once charged with electricity, past a guard tower, and down a long flight of open steps to a small, red brick building—the crematorium. A gentle rain was beginning to fall. Two American soldiers stationed in Germany were there. One had read Bonhoeffer's books and had brought his friend with him to see the place where he had died. Behind the crematorium was a mound of earth.

After Bonhoeffer was hanged, his body was carried down those steps to the crematorium and stretched out on a steel table. That table is still there as a grim reminder of demonic efficiency. His hair was shaved, and the gold fillings removed from his teeth. Then his body was shoved into the oven. His ashes now rest beneath the grass of that common mound, the final resting place of an unknown number of men, most of whom are forever nameless.

There is a chapel beyond the mound of human ashes, constructed of stones from the guard towers that once overlooked the perimeters of that labor camp. In the chancel is a massive crucifix. The anguished face of the Savior is unforgettable, as if a scream of outrage is about to burst from his lungs. On the right side of the Crucified One, beneath his piniored right arm are two figures: one an inmate, a Jew from Poland, perhaps, who worked the granite mines at Flossenburg; the other, a guard who stands over him with a whip. On the left side of the Crucified stands the figure of a woman bearing a heavy load and shielding a little child. It is as if the arms of the Crucified reach out over the tormented and the tormenter, over Christian, Jew, and unbeliever alike.

The rain had stopped as we left the chapel. The sun was out and birds were singing. We all walked singly and silently back to the bus. And as the bus pulled away, the leader of our seminar, Theodore A. Gill, close friend of the Bonhoeffer family, did the thing we all felt had to be done. He led us in prayer. It was a simple prayer, thanking God for those who live among us from time to time who are too good for this world to hold.

Can I fully explain why and how this visit to Flossenburg touched something deep within me? Maybe it had something to do with the fact that my father's people were Bavarian, and it was like being drawn to mystic roots. Or maybe it was because my father died of a heart attack on Tuesday, April 10, 1945, a few hours after Dietrich Bonhoeffer was hanged. Somehow that personal loss that left an indelible mark on me is strangely attached to the loss of that great hero of the church. Or maybe it's that early in my ministry the writings of Bonhoeffer made a lasting impression on me and helped shape my theological outlook. Many have been so influenced by this martyr. There was a lady in our group, superintendent of schools in Montclair, New Jersey. On the night when Bonhoeffer's niece, Renate Bethge, spoke to our seminar, this lady stood up to say that when she was a student at Union Theological Seminary in New York City, she read Bonhoeffer's *Letters from Prison*, and it changed her life. I understand. How often I return to that same little book, a collection of letters, fragments of sermons, meditative insights, poems, outlines of books he hoped to write—all smuggled out of prison to friends and relatives. This and much more I am not even aware of made this visit a spiritual pilgrimage I will never forget.

We are strange creatures. In each of us is something saintly and some-thing sinister. We are all wise and foolish, fearless and cowardly, strong and weak. We are created to reach for the stars, and beyond the stars to rest in the deathless embrace of the God who made us for himself. But how easily we forget who we are and why we are here. We become preoccupied with so many things: enough money, a new car, whether we'll be comfortably fixed in our retirement, a larger house, whether our children will be financially successful, what political party is in power—as if these are the things that really matter. But from time to time there come into the horizon of our lives those strange individuals, too good for this world to hold, whose lives, whether brief or long, remind us that before all else we belong to God, our eternal dwelling place. Like the Christ he served until death, Dietrich Bonhoeffer's life will not let us forget that we are God's own possession and are given to this world for a moment in time to serve him.

Endnotes

1. Clothing for the Soul
1. Cornelius Plantinga, Jr., *Not the Way It's Supposed to Be* (William B. Eerdmans Publishing Co., Grand Rapids, Mich., 1995), p. 31.
2. Ibid., pp. 31–32.
3. Ibid., p. 32.
4. 1 Peter 2:9.

2. Quiet Agents of Grace
1. Hugh T. Kerr, *The Simple Gospel* (Westminster Press, Louisville, Ky., 1991), p. 65.
2. Cited by Harry Emerson Fosdick in *Successful Fund Raising Sermons*, edited by Julius King (Funk and Wagnalls Co., New York, 1953), p. 53.
3. Cited in *The Interpreter's Bible* (Abingdon Press, Nashville, Tenn., 1954), Vol. 7, p. 283.
4. Acts 10:38.
5. John 4:4–42.
6. Kerr, *The Simple Gospel*, op cit., p. 43.
7. Hebrews 9:11.

3. On Giving Hilariously
1. King, *Successful Fund Raising Sermons*, op cit., p. 108.
2. Edmund Stiemle, *Are You Looking for God?* (Muhlenberg Press, Philadelphia, Pa., 1957), p. 147.
3. Thomas F. Torrence, *Preaching Christ Today* (William B. Eerdmans Publishing Co., Grand Rapids, Mich., 1994), p. 28.
4. Stiemle, *Are You Looking for God?*, op cit., p. 148.
5. Paul Scherer, *Love Is a Spendthrift* (Harper & Bros., New York, 1961), p. 210.
6. Luke 18:11.

4. From Anger to Cynicism

1. These comments by Russell Baker are taken from an article, "Wisdom to Take Along the Way," which appeared in *The Christian Science Monitor*, Monday, June 19, 1995.

2. *Newsweek*, July 10, 1995, p. 27.

3. Baker, op cit.

4. "O God, the wind of whose Spirit bloweth where it listeth, and whose rain falleth where it will: Quicken our ears to hear and our eyes to see the signs of Thy presence, not only where our habits and conventions expect them, but wherever Thy bounty bestows them. So shall our lives be gladdened by every miracle of grace, and our wills be alert to praise Thy goodness to every creature; for His name's sake who was born of the Spirit, the only Saviour of the world. Amen." (*The Book of Common Worship*, Board of Christian Education of the Presbyterian Church, Philadelphia, Pa., 1946), p. 341.

5. Acts 10:38.

5. No One Comes to the Father But by Me

1. For a further discussion of this point, see J. A. DiNoia's article in *Either/Or, The Gospel or Neopaganism* (William B. Eerdmans Publishing Co., Grand Rapids, Mich., 1995), chap. 3.

2. T. W. Manson, *The Teachings of Jesus* (Cambridge University Press, London, England, 1951), p. 101.

3. Ibid., p. 93.

4. Mark 8:27–30; Matthew 16:13–20; Luke 9:18–22.

5. For a full discussion of the way we corrupt religion, see Jacques Ellul, *Living Faith* (Harper & Row Publishers, San Fransisco, Calif., 1983), p. 153.

6. From the hymn, "Jesus, the Very Thought of Thee," an eleventh-century Latin hymn.

6. On Being Responsible for Our Lives

1. Cited by O. Hobart Mowrer in *The Crisis in Psychiatry and Religion* (D. Van Nostrand Co., Inc., Princeton, N.J., 1961), p. 49.

2. Matthew 11:28–30.

7. Life Can Begin Again

1. John H. Leith, *The Reformed Imperative* (The Westminster Press, Philadelphia, Pa., 1988), p. 96.

2. Helmut Thielicke, *Life Can Begin Again* (Fortress Press, Philadelphia, Pa., 1956), p. xii.

3. Leith, *The Reformed Imperative*, op cit., p. 91.

4. From the hymn, "Jesus the Very Thought Of Thee."
5. W. H. Auden, *The Age of Anxiety* (Random House, New York, 1847), p. 134.

8. Three Popular Misunderstandings of Faith
1. Cited by James W. Van Hoeven, writing in *Perspectives* (Reformed Church Press, Grand Rapids, Mich.), June/July, 1994.
2. Helmut Thielicke, *The Waiting Father* (Harper & Bros., New York, 1959), p. 74.
3. *Creative Suffering, The Ripple of Hope* (Pilgrim Press, Kansas City, Mo., 1970), pp. 119 and 121.

9. Who Needs a Savior?
1. Gordon D. Marino, "The Epidemic of Forgiveness," *Commonweal* (Commonweal Foundation, New York), March 24, 1995, p. 9.
2. Plantinga, *Not the Way It's Supposed to Be, A Breviary of Sin*, op cit., p. 198.
3. See the article by Jonathan Alter and Pat Wingert, "The Return of Shame," *Newsweek*, Feb. 6, 1995.
4. John Leo in *Commonweal*, op cit., Feb. 24, 1995, p. 45.
5. *Commonweal*, op cit., March 24, 1995, p. 11.
6. Ibid., p. 10.
7. Luke 23:34.

10. Hearing the Gospel for the First Time
1. Jacques Ellul, *This I Believe* (William B. Eerdmans, Grand Rapids, Mich., 1989), p. 57.
2. Torrence, *Preaching Christ Today*, op cit., p. 34.
3. Ian Maclearen, *Beside the Bonnie Brier Bush* (Hodder and Stoughton, London, England, 1894).

11. God's Agenda and Ours
1. Sherer, *Love Is a Spendthrift*, op cit., p. 199.
2. From *The Riddle of Joy*, edited by Michael H. Macdonald and Andrew A. Tadie, (William B. Eerdmans, Grand Rapids, Mich., 1989), p. 90.

12. A Maundy Thursday Homily
1. John Baillie, *A Dairy of Private Prayer* (Charles Scribner's Sons, New York, 1949), p. 59.

13. A Theological Question About Health Care
1. Democratic Senator William Mitchell of Maine. So complex became the health care debate that it was subsequently dropped by the 1994 Congress.
2. Steven Waldman, *Newsweek*, July 25, 1994, p. 19.
3. *Commonweal*, op cit., July 25, 1994, p. 3.
4. From an article by Dr. J. Hayden Hollingsworth, president of the Virginia Chapter of the American College of Cardiology.
5. Lamar Williamson, Jr., in his commentary on Mark in the *Interpretation* Series (John Knox Press, Louisville, Ky., 1983), p. 65.

14. Life Work
1. Donald Hall, *Life Work* (Beacon Press, Boston, Mass., 1993).
2. Ibid., p. 54.
3. Matthew 6:2.
4. From Isaac Watts' memorable hymn based on the 90th Psalm, "O God, Our Help in Ages Past."

15. Reformed Spirituality
1. Howard L. Rice, *Reformed Spirituality* (Westminster/John Knox Press, Louisville, Ky., 1991), p. 7.
2. Ibid., p. 21.
3. Daniel L. Migliore, *Faith Seeking Understanding* (William B. Eerdmans Publishing Co., Grand Rapids, Mich., 1991), p. 2.
4. Ibid., p. 5.
5. *Context* (Claretian Publications, Chicago, Ill.,) April 1, 1993.
6. Hughes Oliphant Old in an article, "What Is Reformed Spirituality?" which appeared in the January 1994 issue of *Perspectives* (Reformed Church Press, Grand Rapids, Mich.), p. 8.
7. John H. Leith *An Introduction to the Reformed Tradition* (John Knox Press, Atlanta, Ga., 1977), p. 69.

16. The Promise of Christmas
1. 2 Corinthians 5:19.
2. Paul Scherer, *The Word God Sent* (Harper & Row, Publishers, New York, 1965), p. 192.

17. Understanding the Gospel
1. Kent R. Hill, writing about the famous Christian apologist, Gilbert K. Chesterton, argues that one of the great obstacles in the way of understanding the gospel is widespread misunderstanding of the most basic

Christian beliefs. " . . . before an individual can consider whether to accept Christian thruths, a plethora of modern misunderstandings and distortions regarding orthodoxy must be dispelled. The task of dispelling common myths about Christianity has become increasingly difficult as contemporary education has become increasingly vacuous. Religion and values have been pushed further and further to the periphery in order to advance an allegedly neutral agenda of pluralism. . . . If in the contemporary world the con-frontation with Christian truth has been rendered particularly difficult because its central claims are not even understood, then a modern apologist (like Chesterton) will have to give specific attention to this obstacle to the acquisition of faith." (From the book, *The Riddle of Joy*, op cit., pp. 226-227).

2. I was introduced to Pascal's analysis by Diogenes Allen in his book, *Christian Belief in a Postmodern World* (Westminster/John Knox Press, Louisville, Ky., 1989).

3. Ibid., p. 109.

4. Ibid., pp. 109-110.

5. Ibid., p. 110.

6. Ibid., p. 225.

18. A Colony of Heaven

1. *Context*, op cit., November 15, 1993.

2. Ibid.

3. G. B. Caird, *The Truth of the Gospel*, Part III of a trilogy, *A Primer of Christianity* (Oxford University Press, London, New York, Toronto, 1950), p. 157.

4. 1 John 4:20.

19. The Sacred Limits Others Pose for Us

1. Genesis 2:18.

2. Cited by Nathan A. Scott, Jr., in his book *Mirrors of Man in Existentialism* (Abingdon Press, Nashville, Tenn., 1978), p. 175.

3. Dietrich Bonhoeffer, *Creation and Fall* (The Macmillan Co., New York, 1959), p. 79.

4. Allen, *Christian Belief in a Postmodern World*, op cit., pp. 105-111.

5. Ibid., p. 107.

6. See Romans 1:29.

20. The Influence of Noble Human Beings

1. Cited in *Voices of Protest and Hope*, compiled by Elisabeth D. Dodds (Friendship Press, New York, 1965), p. 145.

2. *Creative Suffering*, op cit.
3. Ibid., p. 14.
4. John 1:14.
5. Isaiah 5:20.
6. Luke 10:16.

21. A Visit to Flossenburg

1. It is interesting to note that recent neurological studies which have mapped the anatomy of the human brain indicate that Professor Bonhoeffer was on the right track and that Sigmund Freud, for all his valuable insights, was pursuing the wrong path.